PENGUIN

A Taste of the Sun

ELIZABETH DAVID (1913–1992) was a legendary writer and cook. Living in Greece at the outbreak of the Second World War, she did not return to Britain until peace was declared. She found the country worn down by rationing and dull food. In 1950 she published *Mediterranean Food*, which, along with subsequent books including *Italian Food* and *French Provincial Cooking*, changed the face of cookery in Britain for ever. In her later works she explored the traditions of English cooking. She received many honours, including a CBE in 1986. She is widely considered Britain's greatest twentieth-century cookery writer, and her books today continue to inspire many, who find her philosophy of simplicity, authenticity, knowledge and care to their liking.

A Taste of the Sun

ELIZABETH DAVID

PENGUIN BOOKS

PENGUIN BOOKS

Published by the Penguin Group

Penguin Books Ltd, 80 Strand, London WC2R 0RL, England

Penguin Group (USA) Inc., 375 Hudson Street, New York, New York 10014, USA

Penguin Group (Canada), 90 Eglinton Avenue East, Suite 700, Toronto, Ontario,
Canada M4P 2Y3 (a division of Pearson Penguin Canada Inc.)

Penguin Ireland, 25 St Stephen's Green, Dublin 2, Ireland
(a division of Penguin Books Ltd)

Penguin Group (Australia), 250 Camberwell Road,
Camberwell, Victoria 3124, Australia
(a division of Pearson Australia Group Pty Ltd)

Penguin Books India Pvt Ltd, 11 Community Centre,
Panchsheel Park, New Delhi – 110 017, India

Penguin Group (NZ), 67 Apollo Drive, Rosedale, Auckland 0632, New Zealand
(a division of Pearson New Zealand Ltd)

Penguin Books (South Africa) (Pty) Ltd, 24 Sturdee Avenue,
Rosebank, Johannesburg 2196, South Africa

Penguin Books Ltd, Registered Offices: 80 Strand, London WC2R 0RL, England

www.penguin.com

This collection published in Penguin Books 2011

1

Copyright © the Estate of Elizabeth David, 2011
All rights reserved

These extracts have previously been published in *French Country Cooking, Of Pageants
and Picnics, Italian Food, Is There a Nutmeg in the House?, French Provincial Cooking,
English Bread and Yeast Cookery* and *An Omelette and a Glass of Wine*, all published by
Penguin Books

Set in 10.75/13 pt Berkeley Oldstyle Book
Typeset by by Jouve (UK), Milton Keynes
Printed in Great Britain by Clays Ltd, St Ives plc

Cover design based on a pattern from a Chequers design plate by Terence Conran for
Midwinter Modern, *c.* 1954. (Photograph copyright © Victoria & Albert Museum.)
Picture research by Samantha Johnson. Lettering by Stephen Raw

ISBN: 978-0-241-95108-8

www.greenpenguin.co.uk

Contents

USEFUL ADVICE

Batterie de Cuisine

Delicious meals can, as everybody knows, be cooked with the sole aid of a blackened frying-pan over a primus stove, a camp fire, a gas-ring or even a methylated spirit lamp. This book, however, is for those whose ambitions lie in the direction of something less primitive in the way of food, so the question of stocking the kitchen with good pans and the right implements is of the first importance.

If you are starting from scratch, the most satisfactory method is to see that you have the basic necessities to begin with and buy gradually as you find out which style of cooking best suits your talents. (If, for example, you have no particular flair for cakes and pastries, it is pointless to clutter up the kitchen with a whole range of pastry boards, cake tins, tartlet moulds and icing sets.)

One thing is quite certain, and that is that if Englishwomen paid more attention to having the right equipment in their kitchens, we should hear a great deal less about the terrible labour of good cooking. How many times have I been told: 'Oh, I haven't time to fiddle about with that kind of thing', just because a recipe called for putting something through a sieve or chopping up a few vegetables. Don't hamper your cooking and waste time and materials through lack of the right tools for the job.

First, and these are essential to any kitchen, come the very best quality of cook's knives. You need a small vegetable knife, razor sharp, a medium one for trimming meat and fish (known as a filleting knife), a large one for cutting up meat and poultry, and a long, thin-bladed ham knife for cold meat, and anything which has to be thinly sliced. A first-class bread knife goes without saying; keep it for bread. Take the greatest care of your knives; don't cut with them on an enamel or marble-topped table or a plate; have a good steel for sharpening; keep your kitchen knives in a special box or compartment of the knife drawer; wash, dry, and put them away, with the points stuck into a cork, as soon as you have finished with them. Let it be understood by all members of the household that there will be serious trouble if your knives are borrowed for screwdriving, prising open packing-cases, cutting fuse wire or any other purpose for which they were not intended.

[. . .]

A straightforward saucepan of 1–2 pint capacity, of heavy quality and with a well-balanced handle, is an asset to anyone who intends to practise serious sauce-making. If this pan is to be a copper one, it is important that the tinning be kept in good condition, so for stirring use a wooden spoon or spatula rather than a whisk which scratches and quickly wears out the tin.

The more experienced cook, progressing to specialized work, may want to invest in the traditional untinned hemispherical copper egg bowl which is unequalled for the successful beating of egg whites but not easy to keep in immaculate condition. An untinned heavy quality (and unless it is heavy quality, a minimum of one-sixteenth of an inch thick, don't bother with it) preserving pan is another worthwhile buy, and so, for the ambitious pastry cook or confectioner, is an untinned, lipped, sugar-boiling pan. It should be noted that it is because the melting point of tin is lower than the boiling point of sugar that copper pans for jam-making, confectionery and sugar-work generally are never tinned. To clean untinned copper, rub with a cut lemon dipped in fine salt, or with a soft rag dipped in a strong solution of vinegar and salt.

[. . .]

Heavy copper, cast aluminium, and cast iron pans with machine-turned bases are all suitable for all types of cooking stoves. So is stainless steel, but it is a bad heat conductor and to be efficient a stainless steel pan must be heavily copper-clad on the base, which makes for enormous and, it seems to me, unnecessary expense.

Whether you choose cast aluminium, enamelled steel, tinned copper, enamelled cast iron or stainless steel, be sure to have at least two deep stew pans, one large and one small, with a small handle at each side; in these all manner of soups and stews can be put in the oven as well as on top of the stove, an essential requirement for anyone who has other duties than those of a cook to attend to. For boiling potatoes keep one special pan with an enamel lining. Another essential is a shallow oval or round fire-proof pan which will go under the grill or in a very hot oven for dishes which are to be browned quickly. One large pan of a minimum 1½ gallon capacity is a necessity for cooking rice and spaghetti, and for anything over four people you must have a still larger one, say 2 to 3 gallons' capacity, and this will do for the boiling of chickens and for making stock. Shallow, two-handled pots from seven to ten inches in diameter and about three inches deep for risotto, pot roasts, various forms of ragoûts and vegetable dishes are a blessing. These can be found in copper, cast aluminium or, better still, enamel-lined cast iron with machine-turned bases.

Earthenware casseroles and terrines for oven cooking should be in every household; for some of the French farmhouse and peasant dishes described in this book they are essential; cassoulets, choux farçis, daubes and civets, lose something of their flavour and a good deal of their charm if cooked in an ordinary saucepan. Earthenware pots can be put on the top of gas and electric stoves, provided an asbestos mat or the more solid modern fire-clay simmer-plate is put underneath. The important point to remember is never to pour cold water into one of these casseroles while it is hot, or it will crack.

For eggs, good frying and omelette pans are obviously needed, and little dishes for eggs en cocotte. Plain white, fireproof porcelain or glass egg-dishes can be found in various sizes, and these are the most satisfactory for baked eggs and eggs *sur le plat*, as the egg does not stick as it does to earthenware. The larger sizes are useful for an infinite variety of little dishes. Three frying-pans and one omelette pan are not too many, and they should all be heavy, with a perfectly flat bottom, or the food will never be evenly fried. Have one general-purpose ten- to twelve-inch frying-pan, preferably with a lip so that it is easy to pour off the fat; one which is kept for steaks and

cutlets and so on; one small one (say six inches) for frying a few croûtons for soup or anything else to be done
in small quantities.

Heavy wrought-iron pans with curved inner walls are
still used for the cooking of omelettes and for many
other routine frying purposes in most households and in
every restaurant in France. Professional chefs, however
firm their attachment to copper stewpans and sauce-
pans, do not use copper omelette pans except for the
table-lamp cooking of *crêpes Suzette*, steak Diane and
similar flambé dishes. Iron pans for omelettes or restaurant frying are now imported in some quantity from
France. English-made frying-pans of the same type are
to be approached with caution. Although cheap they are
often unsatisfactory because the manufacturers have
failed to grasp the importance of balance where the
weight and the angle of the handles are concerned. A
frying-pan with an over-heavy handle looks and feels
impressive in the hand but topples sideways when put
on the stove, and to the household cook is just one more
source of unnecessary aggravation.

A certain amount of superstition still hangs about the
so-called 'proving' and maintenance of iron pans. There
are still those who recommend that a new pan be rubbed
with coarse salt (a first-class way of ensuring instant
wreckage of a new pan) or be filled with salt and water
to be left boiling for an hour or two. Such advice should
not be taken seriously. Salt corrodes, pits, and discolours
the burnished metal. Perhaps it is not generally understood that when these pans leave the factory they are
coated with a protective film of grease which should be

left undisturbed until the pan reaches the customer's kitchen. A preliminary cleaning with a rag, detergent, and hot water removes the superficial grease and any remainder is easily dealt with by heating a generous amount of oil or lard in the pan for a few minutes. Leave this to cool, pour it off, rub the pan clean with newspaper or kitchen tissues, and dry it thoroughly. Once cleaned of its grease the pan is used like any other pan, but when not in use should be kept greased or oiled so that the risk of rust is eliminated. The legend that an iron omelette pan should never be washed owes its origin and perpetuation to this risk and to the high incidence of scratching and scoring induced by drastic scouring, incomplete drying, consequent rust spots, and eventual ruination of the smooth surface of the pan.

Because a correctly made omelette comes away clean from the pan, a pan used and kept exclusively for omelettes by a deft cook does not require washing. Should the necessity arise (and it is unrealistic to assume that we are all perfectly accomplished cooks all of the time) it is infinitely preferable to give your pan a mild scrub in soap and water than to scrape away at it with a knife or savage it with coarse wire wool (fine steel wool should do no harm, but a well-worn Scotch-Brite or Scat pad is better) in the mistaken belief that so long as no water touches your pan no harm can come to it. Whatever method of cleaning is adopted, whether it is a quick rinse or a rub with paper, remember to dry the pan thoroughly and unless it is in daily use to brush the inside with a film of oil or fat before it is put away. The same treatment should be applied to iron paëlla pans and pancake pans.

Anyone who feels that there is too much palaver involved in the regular use of an iron frying-pan would perhaps do best to invest in a heavy cast aluminium all-purpose frying-pan and keep an iron pan only for omelettes. Personally, I use cast aluminium, French en-amelled cast-iron and plain iron with impartiality and do not reserve one pan exclusively for omelettes.

For a two-egg omelette, use a 6 to 7 inch pan, for three eggs a 9 to 10 inch pan, for five eggs a 12 inch pan. After that, unless you are a professional omelette cook, make two or three omelettes rather than attempt the tricky task of making a gigantic omelette in a 14 to 15 inch pan which, however well-proportioned, is cumbersome and unwieldy until you become accustomed to the handling of large and heavy pans.

A deep frier with a basket is necessary for chips and for the deep frying of fritters and fish, and for lifting fried food out of the pan you need a perforated ladle or wire skimmer.

[. . .]

For poaching a whole large fish, such as salmon or an outsize bass, you need a long narrow fish-kettle with an inner drainer on which the fish rests, so that it can be lifted out of the pan and drained without fear of breakage. Fish kettles are expensive, but are to be found now and again at sales and in junk shops. Oval gratin dishes in varying sizes for baking and grilling fish are easy to find, in earthenware, china or metal, or enamel-lined cast iron. A long platter for serving fish is important; the appearance of a fine salmon, trout or bass is ruined by being brought to table on too small a dish.

The question of kitchen tools is one which must depend on personal preferences, and I cannot do more than enumerate those which through long use and the saving of countless hours I regard with especial affection.

First of these is a purée-maker or food mill. For soups, sauces, fruit and vegetable purées this is absolutely invaluable; in two minutes you have a purée which would take 30 minutes' bashing to get through an ordinary sieve. The best and cheapest of these is a French one, called the *mouli*, and the medium size, about £1.50, is the one for a small household. Even if you have an electric blender you will probably find that you still need, and use, a *mouli*. Then there is a vegetable slicer which goes by the charming name of *mandoline*. If you have ever spent an hour slicing a cucumber paper-thin, or cutting potatoes for *pommes Anna* or *pommes soufflés*, go and buy one of these – a whole cucumber can be done, thinner than you could ever do it with a knife, in a minute or two.

Vegetable choppers are now obtainable in England; called in France a *hachoir*, in Italy a *mezzaluna*, these instruments are crescent-shaped blades with a handle at each end. They make the fine chopping of onions, meat, parsley and vegetables the affair of a second. For small quantities of parsley and other fresh herbs a solid wooden bowl with its own crescent-bladed knife is invaluable. This is called a *hachinette*.

Electric mixers, mincers, vegetable shredders and potato peelers proliferate on the market. For the small household and for beginners the French Moulinex machines offer the best value, the widest choice and the maximum ingenuity. Their recently introduced Mouli-nette automatic chopper is a particularly valuable machine which performs just what it promises. That is, it chops raw as well as cooked meats without squeezing out their juices or turning them into an emulsion. The new Mouli large-capacity electrical potato peelers are useful if not precisely beautiful.

A good pair of scales, a measuring jug, a first-class pliable stainless steel palette knife, a perforated slice, a pepper mill and a salt mill are obvious necessities; so is a selection of wooden spoons and a pair of kitchen scissors, two or three fine strainers in different sizes, and a clock. A perforated spoon for draining anything which has cooked in deep fat is a great boon; a good solid chopping-board, at least twelve inches by eighteen inches, you must have, and either a wood or marble pestle and mortar.

A rather large selection of cooking and mixing bowls I insist on having – there can't be too many in any kitchen – and the same goes for a collection of air-tight plastic boxes for storing vegetables, salads and fresh herbs in the refrigerator. A supply of muslin squares for draining home-made cheese and for straining aspic jelly, an extra plate rack for saucepan lids, some ovenproof plates and serving dishes, glass store jars in all sizes and a supply of heavy quality greaseproof paper are all adjuncts of a good working kitchen. Aluminium foil we now take for granted, but less well known, and very clean and satisfactory for storage as well as for cooking, are Porosan bags – also ideal, incidentally, as sandwich and picnic food wrappers.

As time goes on you accumulate your own personal gadgets, things which graft themselves on to your life; an ancient thin-pronged fork for the testing of meat, a broken knife for scraping mussels, a battered little copper saucepan in which your sauces have always turned out well, an oyster knife which you can no longer afford to use for its intended purpose but which turns out to be just the thing for breaking off hunks of Parmesan cheese, a pre-war sixpenny tin-opener which has outlived all other and superior forms of tin-opening life, an earthenware bean-pot of such charm that nothing cooked in it could possibly go wrong.

Some sensible person once remarked that you spend the whole of your life either in your bed or your shoes. Having done the best you can by shoes and bed, devote all the time and resources at your disposal to the building up of a fine kitchen. It will be, as it should be, the most comforting and comfortable room in the house.

Wine in the Kitchen

Nobody has ever been able to find out why the English regard a glass of wine added to a soup or stew as a reckless foreign extravagance and at the same time spend pounds on bottled sauces, gravy powders, soup cubes, ketchups and artificial flavourings. If every kitchen contained a bottle each of red wine, white wine, and inexpensive port for cooking, hundreds of store cupboards could be swept clean for ever of the cluttering debris of commercial sauce bottles and all synthetic aids to flavouring.

To the basic sum of red, white and port I would add, if possible, brandy, and half a dozen miniature bottles of assorted liqueurs for flavouring sweet dishes and fruit salads, say Kirsch, Apricot Brandy, Grand Marnier, Orange Curaçao, Cointreau and Framboise. Sherry is a good addition, but should be used in cooking with the utmost discretion; it is vain to think that the addition of a large glass of poor sherry to the contents of a tin of soup is going to disguise it.

THE COOKING OF WINE

The fundamental fact to remember about the use of wine in cooking is that the wine is *cooked*. In the process the alcohol is volatilized and what remains is the wonderful flavour which perfumes the dish and fills the kitchen with an aroma of delicious things to come. In any dish which does not require long cooking the wine should be reduced to about half the quantity originally poured in the pan, by the process of very fast boiling. In certain soups, for instance, when the vegetables have been browned and the herbs and spices added, a glass of wine is poured in, the flame turned up, and the wine allowed to bubble fiercely for two or three minutes; when it starts to look a little syrupy on the bottom of the pan, add the water or stock; this process makes all the difference to the flavour and immediately gives the soup body and colour.

When making gravy for a roast, abolish the cabbage water, gravy browning and cornflour; instead, when you have strained off the fat pour a ½ glass of any wine round the roasting-pan, at the same time scraping up all the juice which has come out of the meat, let it sizzle for a minute or two, add a little water, cook gently another 2 minutes and your gravy is ready.

For a duck, add the juice of an orange and a tablespoon of red-currant jelly; for fish which has been grilled add white wine to the butter in the pan, lemon juice, and chopped parsley or capers; to the butter in which you have fried escalopes of veal add a little red wine or Madeira, let it bubble and then pour in a ½ cup of cream.

TO FLAMBER

To *flamber* is to set light to a small quantity of brandy, liqueur or rum poured over the contents of the pan, which are left to flame until the alcohol has burnt away, leaving a delicately composed sauce in which any excess of fat or butter has been consumed in the flames. The brandy or liqueur will be easier to light if it is first placed in a warmed ladle, to release the spirit, which will then easily catch fire.

TO MARINATE IN WINE

To marinate meat, fish or game is to give it a bath lasting anything between 2 hours and several days in a marinade usually composed of a mixture of wine, herbs, garlic, onions and spices, sometimes with the addition of a little vinegar, olive oil, or water. A tough piece of stewing beef is improved by being left several hours in a marinade of red wine; it can then be braised or stewed in the marinade, strained of the vegetables and herbs which, by this time, have become sodden, and fresh ones added.

A leg of mutton can be given a taste approximating to venison by being marinaded for several days. It is then carefully dried and roasted, the strained marinade being reduced and used for the sauce.

For certain *terrines* I always marinate the prepared meat or game for two or three hours in white wine, but red can be used. Hare, I think, needs no marinade, unless it is ancient and tough, as the meat of a good hare has a perfect flavour which is entirely altered by being soaked in wine before cooking, although a glass or two of good red wine to French *civet de lièvre*, and of port to English jugged hare, is indispensable.

THE CHOICE OF THE WINE

There is no hard-and-fast rule as to the use of white or red wine, port or brandy for any particular dish. Generally speaking, of course, red wine is better for meat and game dishes, white for fish, but one can usually be substituted for the other, an exception being *Moules Marinière*, for which white wine is a necessity, as red turns the whole dish a rather disagreeable blue colour, and any essentially white dish, such as a delicate concoction of sole, must have white wine.

Incidentally, white wine for cooking should, except for certain dishes such as a cheese fondue, not be too dry, as it may give rather too acid a flavour; and beware of pouring white wine into any sauce containing milk or cream; to avoid curdling, the wine should be put in before the cream and well simmered to reduce the acidity, and the cream stirred in off the fire, and reheated very cautiously.

Don't be discouraged when you read lovely French regional recipes containing a particular and possibly little-known wine; remember that in their country of origin the *vin du pays* is always within arm's reach of the cook, so that while in Bordeaux a *Matelote* of eel is cooked in wine of the Médoc, in Lyons the nuance is altered because Beaujolais is used, and cider in the apple country of Normandy. Here, too, a sweet omelette is *flambéd* with Calvados, in Gascony with Armagnac. In the same way the French frequently employ their own sweet wine, Frontignan, Muscat, or the Vin Cuit of Provence in place of port or marsala.

Cider is excellent for white fish, mussels, for cooking ham, and for rabbit, but it should be either draught or vintage cider.

Cheap wine is better than no wine at all, at any rate for cooking, but the better the wine the better the dish. By this I do not mean that fine old vintages should be poured into the saucepan, but that, for instance, Coq au Vin, cooked in a pint of sound Mâcon or Beaujolais, will be a much finer dish than that cooked in fiery Algerian wine.

If you are going to keep wine especially for cooking, it can be bought in half- or even quarter-bottles.

LIQUEURS

A variety of liqueurs in ounce bottles can be bought by the dozen. A word of warning here – liqueurs in fruit salads should be used with some caution and not mixed too freely, or the fruit will simply be sodden and taste like perfumed cotton-wool.

For soufflés use rather more than you think is needed – the taste evaporates with the cooking. Grand Marnier, Mirabelle and Orange Curaçao are particularly good for soufflés and for omelettes and, owing to their concentrated strength, can be used when a wine such as Madeira or Sauternes would have to be used in too great quantity for the volume of the eggs.

The Menu

A list of menus suitable for spring, autumn, summer and winter, for family luncheons, formal dinners, christening tea parties and buffet suppers can never be more than the vaguest of guides; I should be surprised to hear that anybody had ever followed any cookery book menu in every detail; all that is needed to design a perfectly good meal is a little common sense and the fundamental understanding of the composition of a menu. The restrictions of years of rationing have been the cause of some remarkably unattractive developments in the serving of food in restaurants, but if some ignorant or careless restaurant managers still serve chips with spaghetti or boiled potatoes and cauliflowers heaped up in the same dish with curry and rice there is no need for us to do likewise at home; we can plan our dinners round three, or at most four, courses, each one perfect of its kind. In the days of long dinners there were usually two choices at every course, and white and brown succeeded each other monotonously. The idea was right – contrast is important but contrast in texture and the manner of cooking is more essential than the colour, which was frequently arranged so that roast beef with brown gravy was followed by roast chicken with a white sauce and so on through endless expensively dull food.

Whether or not you are your own cook, it is unwise to have more than one course needing last-minute preparation. When opening the meal with a hot soup, it is perfectly reasonable to follow it with a cold main dish, accompanied perhaps by hot baked potatoes. A dish of hot vegetables, which have been braising in butter in the meantime, can succeed the main course, to be followed by a cold sweet. A cold first course can come before a hot dish, which will be simmering in the oven without being spoilt, and can be brought to table with the minimum of fuss. You can then have a cold sweet, and perhaps a savoury, although the savouries acceptable at a dinner party are extremely few, should be very hot and preferably composed of cheese. None of the fishy mixtures spread on tough or sodden toast are in the least welcome at the end of a good meal, in fact the only fish savoury which seems to me worth bothering with is the delicious Angels on Horseback, oysters wrapped up in the thinnest slices of bacon, threaded on skewers, grilled, and served on squares of freshly fried bread, which rules them out for the cook hostess who does not wish to leave her guests while she disappears to the kitchen for ten minutes, emerging breathless and crimson in the face.

Most people can get as far as deciding of what ingredients the meal shall consist, and indeed this is largely dependent on the food in season; the next consideration is the manner of their presentation. A sole cooked in a rich sauce of cream and mushrooms must be followed by a dry dish of entirely different aspect such as a roast partridge or a grilled tournedos, cold ham, jellied beef or a terrine of duck. It must not be preceded by a creamy mushroom soup, nor followed by chicken cooked in a cream sauce. Have some regard for the digestions of others even if your own resembles that of the ostrich. Should you decide to serve your fish grilled, say with little potatoes and an Hollandaise sauce, don't follow it up with another dish requiring potatoes and two more different sauces. The transatlantic manner of serving poultry, game, meat and ham dishes with dozens of different trimmings is simply pointless; the chances are that not one of them will be quite perfectly cooked or sufficiently hot, everybody will have their plates overloaded with half-cold food, and the flavour of the main dish will pass unnoticed amongst the vegetables, relishes, sauces, and salads. One or at most two vegetables are entirely sufficient, and one sauce, nor need potatoes always accompany a meat course. With a roast saddle of hare, for instance, serve a purée of chestnuts, the gravy from the hare, unthickened, but with the addition of a little red wine or port, and perhaps red-currant jelly. Anything else is superfluous. Avoid hot vetegables with anything served in an aspic jelly; if the aspic has been made as it should be with calf's foot and not with artificial gelatine, hot vegetables on the same plate will melt the jelly and make an unattractive watery mess. Potatoes baked in their jackets should be served on separate plates. A delicate green salad, or an orange salad, is the only other accompaniment necessary.

When starting the meal with a hot soufflé avoid serving a mousse at the sweet course; a mousse is only a cold soufflé, and you will have two dishes of exactly the same consistency. In the days of eight courses this was permissible, but with a small meal much more rigid care must be taken.

For the first course, when soup is unsuitable, eggs *en cocotte*, cold poached eggs in aspic, all kinds of *pâté* and terrines, and all the smoked-fish tribe, salmon, trout, eel, cod's roe, and herring are excellent; each accompanied by its particular adjunct, nicely presented hot toast and butter or fresh French bread for the *pâté*, brown bread and butter, lemon and cayenne for the smoked salmon; a creamy horse-radish sauce is the traditional companion of smoked trout, although to my mind this sauce is detrimental to the flavour of the fish.

Any sweets made with cream cheese make a good ending to a luncheon or dinner, particularly for the summer. Being refreshing and light, they are also appropriately served after such aromatic and satisfying dishes as stuffed cabbages. Rich chocolate desserts are better served after very light and simple meals.

For the inexperienced cook it seems fairly obvious to say that it is safer when giving a dinner party to stick to something you know you can do successfully, but this doesn't necessarily mean the food need be stereotyped. A little experimenting beforehand will usually show whether a dish is a suitable one to appear at a party; but showing off, however amiably, may well end in disaster. 'Know your limitations' is a copybook maxim which could be applied more often when planning a meal; many a reputation for skilful entertaining has been founded on the ability to cook one dish to perfection; it may be the flair for doing a rice dish, for roasting a duck, or for poaching eggs. The rest of the meal may consist of salad, fruit and cheese, and it will be infinitely preferable to the over-ambitious menu of several dishes, none of which are quite as they should be.

Deep fried food such as soufflé potatoes, cheese *beignets*, and the delicious *scampi* or Dublin Bay prawns in fritters are better kept for days when you have one or two friends who will eat them with you in the kitchen, straight from the smoking fat, the aroma of which is more penetrating than any other cooking smell, permeating the whole house and your own clothes, so it is not for dressing-up days. It should also be borne in mind by the ambitious cook that many dishes served in grandiose restaurants and designed, in fact, for advertisement are not suitable to the small household. Where there is an army of cooks and waiters it may be admissible to make *Crêpes Suzette* at the table and *flamber* them under your dazzled eyes. At home these conjuring tricks are likely to fall flat. Experience, more than anything else, will bring the ability to plan the cooking and serving so that the minimum anxiety and disturbance at the dinner table is compatible with the maximum excellence of the fare.

[. . .]

A little common sense must be exercised in deciding which dishes can safely be left simmering and which must be served immediately they are ready. It is pointless, for example, to spend time and money on young spring vegetables and then leave them half an hour stewing in the oven; they will have lost all their charm, and it would have been better to serve a purée of dried vegetables. The sterling virtue of punctuality in a cook must give way, if need be, to the greater necessity of keeping guests waiting while last-minute preparations are made.

Picnics

Picnic addicts seem to be roughly divided between those who frankly make elaborate preparations and leave nothing to chance, and those others whose organization is no less complicated but who are more deceitful and pretend that everything will be obtained on the spot and cooked over a woodcutter's fire, conveniently to hand; there are even those, according to Richard Jefferies, who wisely take the precaution of visiting the site of their intended picnic some days beforehand and there burying the champagne.

Not long before the war I was staying with friends in Marseille. One Saturday night a picnic was arranged for the next day with some American acquaintances; it was agreed that the two parties should proceed in their own cars to a little bay outside Marseille, and that we should each bring our own provisions. On Sunday morning I and my friends indulged in a delicious hour of shopping in the wonderful market of the rue de Rome, buying olives, anchovies, salame sausages, pâtés, yards of bread, smoked fish, fruit and cheese. With a provision of cheap red wine we bundled the food into the car and set off, stopping now and again for a drink; so that we arrived at our rendezvous well disposed to appreciate the sun, the sea and the scent of wild herbs and Mediterranean pines. Presently our friends drove up and started to unload their car. One of the first things to come out was a hatchet, with which they efficiently proceeded to chop down olive branches, and in no time at all there was a blazing fire. Out of their baskets came cutlets, potatoes, bacon, skewers, frying pans, jars of ice, butter, table-cloths, all the trappings of a minor barbecue. Our reactions as we watched these proceedings were those of aston-ishment, admiration, and finally, as realization of the inadequacy of our own catering dawned, dismay. How wilted they seemed, those little packets wrapped up in rather oily paper; the olives which had glowed with col-our in the market stalls of the rue de Rome looked shabby now; the salame seemed dried up and the ancho-vies a squalid mess. Miserably, like poor relations, we sat with our shameful bundles spread out on the grass and politely offered them to our friends. They were kind, but obviously preferred their own grilled cutlets and fried potatoes, and we were too embarrassed to accept their proffered hospitality. Presently they produced ice cream out of a thermos, but by now we were past caring, and finally it was their turn for surprise when they found we hadn't even provided ourselves with the means of mak-ing a cup of coffee.

Then there was the hospitable family I remember in my childhood; they owned a beautiful house and an elegant garden and were much given to out-of-door entertainments, pageants and picnics. On picnic days a large party of children and grown-ups would be assem-bled in the hall. Led by our host and hostess we proceeded through the exquisite formal Dutch garden, across the lane and over a fence into a coppice. Close on our heels followed the butler, the chauffeur and the foot-man, bearing fine china plates, the silver and tablecloths, and a number of vast dishes containing cold chickens, jellies and trifles. Arrived at the end of our journey, five minutes from the house, our host set about making a fire, with sticks which I suspect had been strategically placed by the gardener, over which we grilled quantities of sausages and bacon, which were devoured amidst the customary jokes and hilarity. The picnickers' honour thus satisfied, we took our places for an orderly meal, handed round by the footman, and in composition resembling that of an Edwardian wedding breakfast.

Since those days I have had a good many opportun-ities of evolving a picnic technique on the lines laid down by Henry James, 'not so good as to fail of an amusing dis-order, nor yet so bad as to defeat the proper function of repasts'.

Before deciding upon the food, its packing and trans-port must be planned. (I am assuming for the moment a car-transported picnic.) Those who are lucky enough to possess an Edwardian picnic hamper, fitted with spirit lamp and kettle, sandwich tins and a variety of boxes and bottles, need look no further. These hampers may be cumbersome, but they are capacious and solid; an aura of lavish gallivantings and ancient Rolls-Royces hangs about them, and they are infinitely superior to the modern kind in which the use of every inch of space has been planned for you in advance. (At the Lord Roberts workshop in the Brompton Road there are deep square baskets of very solid construction, large enough to hold a good deal of food as well as several bottles, which are still very reasonable in price. This establishment is full of happy ideas for all addicts of eating out of doors, for they sell large hampers, unfitted, so that you can pack whatever you please, baskets with divisions for bottles, baskets for thermos jars, and the most comfortable garden chairs in existence.) Insulated picnic bags are highly effective and useful.

As to plates and glasses, if I am going to have them at all I would prefer to have china plates and glass glasses, although it must be admitted that clear, colourless plastic glasses such as are used on airlines are more practical.

A spirit lamp and kettle plus a tin of Nescafé provide a hotter and fresher cup of coffee than any which ever came out of a vacuum flask. Iced coffee on the other hand can be transported in thermos jugs, and a large thermos jar filled with ice is a blessing for those who don't care for warm drinks, or who like to put ice into coarse red picnic wine.

As for the food, the buying and preparing of it always seem to me to provide half the fun. The possibilities are almost without limit. On the whole, though, I think that such elegant foods as foie gras and lobster patties should be excluded as they seem to lose their fine lustre when eaten out of doors, whereas the simpler charms of salame sausage, fresh cheese, black olives and good French bread (if you can find such a commodity) are enhanced when they are eaten on the hillside or the seashore. Sandwiches I rather like (George Saintsbury considered that venison makes the best sandwiches), but many people do not, so there must always be alternatives; thin slices of ham rolled round Frankfurter sausages, or Frankfurter sausages split in half enclosing a slice of Gruyère cheese are good ones. Remember that such delicious foods as jellied egg, duck in aspic, and so on aren't really ideal for long journeys on a hot day because the jelly (if it has been made as it should be) will melt *en route*; mayonnaise also has a dismaying habit of turning into a rather unappetizing-looking oily mass when the weather is hot. A cold chicken with a cream sauce is a better bid than a chicken mayonnaise. Cold steak and kidney pudding is fine picnic food, so is cold spiced beef, which cuts into nice slices. Cold escalopes of veal, fried in egg and breadcrumbs, make excellent picnic food provided they are very thin and very well drained after frying. Hard-boiled eggs are time-honoured picnic food, so I always take a few, but they are not everybody's taste. Cheese seems to me essential for an out-of-doors meal; next to the salty little Mediterranean goat and sheep's milk cheeses English Cheddar or Cheshire, or Gruyère, are perhaps the easiest picnic cheeses. Some people like a rich moist fruit cake for a picnic, but I prefer a slab of the dryest, bitterest chocolate available (Terry's make a good one but the best is the Belgian Côte d'Or), to be eaten in alternate mouthfuls with a Marie biscuit. Apples and figs and apricots, because they are easy to eat and transport as well as being good in the open air, are perhaps the best fruit for a picnic.

The nicest drinks for picnics are the obvious ones. A stout red wine such as a Mâcon or a Chianti, which cannot be unduly harmed by the journey in the car; vin rosé (particularly delicious by the sea); cider, lager, shandy, Black Velvet; iced sherry and bitters. For a very hot day

Pimm's No. 1 couldn't be bettered but involves some organization in the matter of cucumber, lemonade, oranges, mint, borage, and all the paraphernalia, and a thermos jar of ice is essential. An effective way to keep wine and mineral waters cool on a long journey is to wrap the bottles in several sheets of dampened newspaper.

For soft drinks the most refreshing are tinned grapefruit, orange or pineapple juice, and tomato juice. (In this case include the tin opener.) Delicate china tea, iced, with slices of lemon and mint leaves is admirably reviving. An early edition of Mrs Beeton asserts that 'Water can usually be obtained so it is useless to take it'. For the walker's picnic perhaps the perfect meal has been described by Sir Osbert Sitwell: 'the fruits of the month, cheese with the goaty taste of mountains upon it, and if possible bilberries, apples, raw celery, a meal unsophisticated and pastoral . . .'

ITALIAN DISHES

Pasta Asciutta

On the 15th of November 1930, at a banquet at the restaurant Penna d'Oca in Milan, the famous Italian Futurist poet Marinetti launched his much publicized campaign against all established forms of cooking and, in particular, against *pastasciutta*. 'Futurist cooking', said Marinetti, 'will be liberated from the ancient obsession of weight and volume, and one of its principal aims will be the abolition of *pastasciutta*. *Pastasciutta*, however grateful to the palate, is an obsolete food; it is heavy, brutalizing, and gross; its nutritive qualities are deceptive; it induces scepticism, sloth, and pessimism.'

The day after this diatribe was delivered the Italian press broke into an uproar; all classes participated in the dispute which ensued. Every time *pastasciutta* was served either in a restaurant or a private house interminable arguments arose. One of Marinetti's supporters declared that 'our *pastasciutta*, like our rhetoric, suffices merely to fill the mouth'. Doctors, asked their opinions, were characteristically cautious: 'Habitual and exaggerated consumption of *pastasciutta* is definitely fattening.' 'Heavy consumers of *pastasciutta* have slow and placid characters; meat eaters are quick and aggressive.' 'A question of taste and of the cost of living. In any case, diet should be varied, and should never consist exclusively of one single element.' The Duke of Bovino, Mayor of Naples, plunged into the fight with happy abandon. 'The angels in Paradise,' he affirmed to a reporter, 'eat nothing but *vermicelli al pomodoro*.' To which Marinetti replied that this confirmed his suspicions with regard to the monotony of Paradise and of the life led by the angels.

Marinetti and his friends proceeded to divert themselves and outrage the public with the invention and publication of preposterous new dishes. Most of these were founded on the shock principle of combining unsuitable and exotic ingredients (*mortadella* with nougat, pineapple with sardines, cooked *salame* immersed in a bath of hot black coffee flavoured with eau-de-Cologne, an aphrodisiac drink composed of pineapple juice, eggs, cocoa, caviar, almond paste, red pepper, nutmeg, cloves, and Strega). Meals were to be eaten to the accompaniment of perfumes (warmed, so that the bald-headed should not suffer from the cold), to be sprayed over the diners, who, fork in the right hand, would stroke meanwhile with the left some suitable substance – velvet, silk, or emery paper.

Marinetti's bombshell contained a good deal of common sense; diet and methods of cookery must necessarily evolve at the same time as other habits and customs. But behind this amiable fooling lurked a sinister note: the fascist obsession with nationalism and patriotism, the war to come. 'Spaghetti is no food for fighters.' In the 'conflict to come the victory will be to the swift', '*Pastasciutta* is anti-virile . . . A weighty and encumbered stomach cannot be favourable to physical enthusiasm towards women.' The costly import of foreign flour for *pastasciutta* should be stopped, to boost the national

cultivation of rice. The snobbery of the Italian aristoc-
racy and haute bourgeoisie, who had lost their heads
over American customs, cocktail parties, foreign films,
German music, and French food, was damned by Marinetti as *esterofil* (pro-foreign) and anti-Italian. In future a
bar should be known as a *quisibeve* (here-one-drinks),
a sandwich as a *traidue* (between-two), a cocktail as a
polibibita (multi-drink), the maître-d'hôtel would be
addressed as *guidopalato* (palate-guide), an aphrodisiac
drink was to be called a *guerra in letto* (war-in-the-bed),
a sleeping draught a *pace in letto* (peace-in-the-bed).
Marinetti's tongue was by no means wholly in his cheek.
A message from Mussolini, to be published in *La Cucina
Futurista* (F. Marinetti, 1932), was dedicated 'to my dear
old friend of the first fascist battles, to the intrepid sol-
dier whose indomitable passion for his country has been
consecrated in blood'.

The origin of *pasta* is lost in the mists of antiquity.
There is a popular legend, entirely without foundation,
to the effect that it was introduced into Italy by Marco
Polo on his return from China. The Futurists knew better. *La Cronaca degli memorabilia*, by Dacovio Saraceno,
they claimed, 'is fortunately here to bear witness' that it
is a barbarous legacy from the Ostrogoths who 'frequently and gladly solaced themselves with this food.
The said *macarono* was made from *spelta* (small brown
wheat) and first made its appearance in the reign of the
magnanimous Prince Teodoric in Ravenna, the said
Prince having revealed the secret to Rotufo, his cook.
A kitchen woman, in love with one of the palace guards,
revealed to him the existence of the said *macarono*. From

this beginning the taste for *macarono* spread to the people. They boiled it with onions, garlic and turnips, and licked their fingers and their faces.'

By the end of the Renaissance, according to Marinetti, the wretched macaroni was all but buried in oblivion (although it is on record that Boccaccio liked his macaroni in a sauce of milk and bitter almonds), 'when that noisy rascal of an Aretino once more raised it to the skies; guests who had feasted at his table, to ingratiate themselves into his favour, composed sonnets and eulogies in praise of the macaroni served at his banquets'.

For the rest, Marinetti's effort was not the first that had been made to reform the Italian diet. In the sixteenth century a Genoese doctor had denounced the abuse of *pasta*. Towards the end of the eighteenth century a campaign was instituted against the consumption of excessive quantities of macaroni. Innumerable volumes from the hands of eminent scientists and men of letters proved unavailing. Not only was the passion for *pastasciutta* too deeply rooted in the tastes of the people, but there was also a widely diffused superstition that macaroni was the antidote to all ills, the universal panacea.

Another effort was made in the first half of the nineteenth century by the scientist Michele Scropetta; he, again, achieved nothing concrete. Had it not been for the war Marinetti's campaign might have achieved a certain success; but however aware enlightened Italians may be of the unsuitability of *pasta* as a daily food, the fact remains that the majority of southern Italians (in the north it is replaced by rice or *polenta*) continue to eat *pastasciutta* at midday and probably some kind of *pasta in brodo* at night. Considering the cost of living, this is not surprising; freshly made *pasta* such as *tagliatelle* and *fettuccine* is cheap and versatile. According to circumstances it may be eaten economically with tomato sauce and cheese, with fresh tomatoes when they are cheap, with butter and cheese, with oil and garlic without cheese. The whole dish will cost rather less than two eggs, is immediately satisfying, and possesses the further advantage that every Italian could prepare a dish of spaghetti blindfold, standing on his head in his sleep.

Figure-conscious Italians claim that no fattening effect is produced by *pasta* provided no meat course is served afterwards; vegetables or a salad, cheese and fruit, are quite sufficient. People mindful of their digestions will also tell you that the wise drink water with their spaghetti and wait until it is finished before starting on the wine.

As to the different varieties of *pasta*, they are countless. The catalogue of one big firm alone gives fifty-two different varieties; and to add to the confusion each province has different names for almost identical kinds of *pasta*. In the following chapter I have endeavoured to describe the main varieties.

There are two main distinctions to be made with regard to genuine Italian *pasta*. There is *pasta fatta in casa* (home-made *pasta*), and the kind which is mass-produced and dried in the factory, sold in packets or by the pound, and which will keep almost indefinitely; this is the *pasta* most familiar to us in England, the best-known brands being imported from Naples, where the quality of the water is said to account for its superiority over *pasta* produced in all other parts of Italy.

When you see the words *pasta di pura semola di grano duro* printed on the label of a packet of spaghetti or other *pasta*, it means that the product is made from fine flour obtained from the cleaned endosperm or heart of the durum (hard) wheat grain; the cream of the wheat, in fact. What we know as semolina is produced in a similar way, but is more coarsely milled.

Some kinds of factory-produced *pasta* are made with eggs (the best with 5 eggs to a kilo), some without. *Pasta* coloured green with spinach is also sold in packets. The Italians have brought the manufacture of *pasta* to a fine art, and the difference between home-made and dried *pasta* is chiefly one of texture. Dried or factory *pasta* must, of course, be cooked for about 15 minutes, whereas freshly made *pasta* takes only about 5 minutes.

In all large Italian towns freshly made *tagliatelle*, *fettuccine*, *vermicelli*, and some stuffed pastes such as *tortellini* and *ravioli*, can be bought in the shops, to be cooked at home the same day. In the restaurants of Rome home-made *fettuccine* are a speciality, but as a matter of fact a great many of these restaurants buy their *fettuccine*, or *tagliatelle*, from the shop round the corner, and so do the cooks in private houses, although every Italian cook can, and does, make her own *pasta* if called upon to do so. I have explained the process to the best of my ability in the chapter which follows. Anyone who has a good hand for pastry – and so many English people have – should be able to master the idea after one or two tries. Spaghetti and macaroni require a special machine, and although as a general rule it is less trouble to use bought *pasta* it is useful to know how to make it, and there are some varieties which cannot easily be bought ready made. There are any number of different sauces to be served with *pasta*, and there are still possibilities to be explored.

Do not, I implore, be influenced against *pasta* by the repugnant concoctions served in restaurants under the name of *spaghetti Napolitaine*, *Bolognese* and the like; a good dish of *pasta* is admirable food for one or two days a week, but it must be cooked with as much care as any other dish. Giuseppe Marotta, the Neapolitan writer, has made the point about spaghetti: 'The important thing is to adapt your dish of spaghetti to circumstances and your state of mind.'

The Cooking and Serving of Pasta

In Italy the amount of *pasta* allowed for each person is 3–4 oz., whether home-made or dried. The latter is usually cooked in a large quantity of boiling salted water, say 6 quarts to 12 oz. of *pasta*. It should be cooked *al dente*, that is, very slightly resistant, and it should be strained without delay. A warmed serving dish should be ready, and the *pasta* should be eaten as soon as it has been prepared.

An alternative, but little known, way of cooking manufactured pasta is to calculate one litre or 1¾ pints of water to every 125 gr. or ¼ lb. of dried *pasta*. Bring the water to the boil; add a tablespoon of salt for every 2 litres or half gallon of water. After it comes back to the boil let it continue boiling for 3 minutes. Turn off the heat, cover the saucepan with a towel and the lid, leave it for 5 to 8 minutes according to the thickness of the *pasta*, e.g. 5 minutes for *spaghettini*, 8 for *maccheroni rigati* which are short tubes, ridged and thick. At the end of this time the *pasta* should be just *al dente*.

I learned this excellent method from the directions given on a packet of Agnesi *pasta* bought in the early 1970s. I find it infinitely preferable to the old-fashioned way.

The addition of a generous lump of butter left to melt on the top of the *pasta* as it is served, or of a little olive oil put into the heated dish before the cooked *pasta* is turned into it, are both valuable improvements. Whether the sauce is served separately or stirred into the *pasta* is a matter of taste.

TAGLIATELLE

Tagliatelle are the most common form of home-made *pasta*. In Rome they are usually called *fettuccine*. To make *pasta* at home it is essential to have either a very large pastry board or marble-topped table, and a long rolling pin. To make *tagliatelle* for six people the ingredients are: 1 lb. of flour (preferably strong unbleached bread flour which has a high gluten content), 2 or 3 eggs, salt, a little water. Pour the flour in a mound on the board, make a well in the middle, and break in the 2 eggs. Add a good teaspoonful of salt and 4 tablespoonfuls of water.

Fold the flour over the eggs and proceed to knead with your hands until the eggs and flour are amalgamated and the paste can be formed into a ball. Having obtained a fairly solid consistency, you continue to knead the paste on the board, holding it with one hand while you roll it from you with the other, with the heel of the palm.

During the process, flour your hands and the board from time to time. After about 10 minutes the dough should have the right somewhat elastic consistency. Divide it into two halves. Now roll out the first half, wrapping it round the rolling-pin, stretching it each time a little more. After each turn round the rolling-pin sprinkle flour over the paste; if it is not quite dry it will stick to the board and the rolling-pin and get torn. After the operation has been repeated nine or ten times the paste is very thin and greatly enlarged, but when you think it is thin enough you will still have to roll it out two or three times more until it is transparent enough for the graining of the wooden board to be visible through it. It will be like a piece of material, and can be picked up exactly as if it were a cloth, laid on a table or over the back of a chair (on a clean cloth) while the other half of the dough is being rolled out. Having finished the second half of the dough, both sheets can be left for 30 minutes. Each one is then rolled up lightly, like a newspaper, and cut, with a sharp knife, across into strips rather less than ¼ in. wide. Spread them all out on a cloth or a flat basket and leave them until it is time to cook them. All that has to be done is to drop them into a large deep pan full of boiling salted water. As soon as they rise to the top, in about 5–7 minutes, they are ready. Drain them, put them into a heated dish with a generous lump of butter, and serve them as hot as possible, either with more butter and plenty of Parmesan cheese or with any of the sauces for *pasta* which are described elsewhere in this book.

As will be fairly clear from this description, although the making of *pasta* is neither an intricate nor highly skilled process, it does require patience and time, and a certain knack which can be acquired.

People who have a gift for making pastry will probably be able to make *pasta* easily; those who are cramped for space or who find the processes of kneading and rolling the dough too irksome will be better advised to buy Italian imported *pasta*, or one of the freshly-made types now available in many delicatessen shops and some supermarkets.

TAGLIATELLE ALLA BOLOGNESE

The cooked *tagliatelle*, or whatever *pasta* is chosen, is mixed with the famous *ragù Bolognese* (below). Fresh butter must be served as well, and plenty of grated Parmesan. This dish of *pasta*, known by name all over the world, is served in such a vast number of astounding ways, all of them incorrect (which would not matter if those ways happened to be successful), that it is a revelation to eat it cooked in the true Bolognese fashion.

RAGÙ

This is the true name of the Bolognese sauce which, in one form or another, has travelled round the world. In Bologna it is served mainly with *lasagne verdi*, but it can go with many other kinds of *pasta*. The ingredients to make enough sauce for six generous helpings of *pasta* are 8 oz. of lean minced beef, 4 oz. of chicken livers, 3 oz. of uncooked ham 'both fat and lean', 1 carrot, 1 onion, 1 small piece of celery, 3 tablespoonfuls of concentrated tomato purée, 1 wineglassful of white wine, 2 wineglassfuls of stock or water, butter, salt and pepper, nutmeg.

Cut the bacon or ham into very small pieces and brown them gently in a small saucepan in about ½ oz. of butter. Add the onion, the carrot, and the celery, all finely chopped. When they have browned, put in the raw minced beef, and then turn it over and over so that it all browns evenly. Now add the chopped chicken livers, and after 2 or 3 minutes the tomato purée, and then the white wine. Season with salt (having regard to the relative saltiness of the ham or bacon), pepper, and a scraping of nutmeg, and add the meat stock or water. Cover the pan and simmer the sauce very gently for 30–40 minutes. Some Bolognese cooks add at the last 1 cupful of cream or milk to the sauce, which makes it smoother. Another traditional variation is the addition of the *ovarine* or unlaid eggs which are found inside the hen, especially in the spring when the hens are laying. They are added at the same time as the chicken livers and form small golden globules when the sauce is finished. When the *ragù* is to be served with spaghetti or *tagliatelle*, mix it with the hot *pasta* in a heated dish so that the *pasta* is thoroughly impregnated with the sauce, and add a good piece of butter before serving. Hand the grated cheese separately.

This is the recipe given me by Zia Nerina, a splendid woman, titanic of proportion but angelic of face and manner, who in the 1950s owned and ran the Trattoria Nerina in Bologna. Zia Nerina's cooking was renowned far beyond the confines of her native city.

LASAGNE VERDI AL FORNO
(Baked Green Lasagne)

Lasagne verdi are large strips of *pasta* coloured green with
spinach. The Bolognese way of cooking them makes a
rich and sustaining dish; a salad and fruit is about all one
can eat after a good helping of *lasagne*. The proportions
for *lasagne verdi* for six are: 1 lb. of flour, 3 eggs, 3 oz.
(weighed when cooked) of purée of spinach, and 2 tea-
spoonfuls of salt. It is most important that the spinach
should be very thoroughly drained before being mixed
with the flour and eggs. Heap the flour up on the pastry
board, make a well in the centre, break in the 3 eggs, add
the salt. With the hands, fold the flour over the eggs and
mix them thoroughly, then add the spinach. This paste
must be thoroughly kneaded and worked, pushing it
away from you on the board with the palms of the hands.
It will be at least 10 minutes before the paste has attained
the required elasticity. Now divide the paste into two
pieces. Flour the board and the rolling pin, and roll out
the dough again and again, stretching it as you do so
round the rolling-pin, pulling it out thinner all the time,
and lightly flouring the flattened paste between each
rolling to keep it from sticking. By the time it has been
rolled and pulled about twelve times it should be like a
piece of cloth which you can fold or roll up in any way
you please without its breaking. Put this prepared paste
over a clean cloth on a table while you work the second
half of the paste. When both are ready, cut them into
pieces about half the size of an ordinary postcard.

Having ready a large pan of boiling water, throw in the *lasagne* and let them cook for 5 minutes. Drain them, and put them into a bowl of cold salted water. You should have ready a *ragù Bolognese* as described on p. 42, and an equal quantity of very creamy béchamel sauce flavoured with nutmeg (nutmeg plays an important part in Bolognese cooking). You also need a wide and fairly deep fireproof dish of earthenware, porcelain, or copper, or a large cake tin. Butter it well, and on the bottom put a first coating of *ragù*, then one of béchamel, then one of *lasagne*. Start again with the *ragù* and béchamel, and continue until the dish is filled, finishing with a layer of *ragù* with the béchamel on the top, and a final generous coating of grated Parmesan cheese.

Put the dish into a previously heated but moderate oven for about 30 minutes. Keep an eye on it to see that the *lasagne* are not drying up, although it is inevitable that they will get slightly crisp around the edges of the dish.

A very adequate dish can be made from bought green *lasagne* or noodles as long as they are of good quality. But beware those English-made green noodles which are artificially coloured. The colour comes out in the water when you cook them. Check the list of ingredients before you buy a packet. The preliminary cooking will take 10–15 minutes instead of 5 minutes; otherwise proceed in the same manner.

SPAGHETTI ALL'AGLIO E OLIO
(*Spaghetti with Oil and Garlic*)

Since the cost of living in Italy is very high, many people cannot now afford meat sauces, butter, or even Parmesan with their daily *pasta*; it is often eaten with no embellish-ment but oil and garlic. Those who are particularly addicted to spaghetti and to garlic will find this dish excellent, others will probably abominate it. It is essen-tial that the oil be olive oil and of good quality. When your spaghetti is cooked, barely warm a cupful of oil in a small pan, and into it stir whatever quantity of finely chopped garlic you fancy. Let it soak in the oil a bare minute, without frying, then stir the whole mixture into the spaghetti. You can add chopped parsley or any other herb, and of course grated cheese if you wish, although the Neapolitans do not serve cheese with spaghetti cooked in this way. If you like the taste of garlic without wishing actually to eat the bulb itself, pour the oil on to the spaghetti through a strainer, leaving the chopped garlic behind.

CHIOCCIOLE AL MASCARPONE E NOCE
(Pasta Shells with Cream Cheese and Walnuts)

Mascarpone is a pure, double-cream cheese made in Northern Italy, sometimes eaten with sugar and strawber-ries in the same way as the French Crémets and Cœur à la Crème. We have several varieties of double-cream cheese here. None has the finesse of *mascarpone* but there are one or two which make a most excellent sauce for *pasta*.

Boil 6 to 8 oz. of *pasta* shells. Some are very hard, and take as long as 20 minutes; and although they are small they need just as large a proportion of water for the cooking as other factory-made *paste*.

The sauce is prepared as follows: in a fire-proof

46

serving dish melt a lump of butter, and for 3 people 4 to 6 oz. of double-cream cheese. It must just gently heat, not boil. Into this mixture put your cooked and drained *pasta*. Turn it round and round adding two or three spoonfuls of grated Parmesan. Add 2 oz. or so (shelled weight) of roughly chopped walnuts. Serve more grated cheese separately.

This is an exquisite dish when well prepared, but it is filling and rich, so a little goes a long way.

Fish Soups

Surely it is curious that this island, with its vast fishing industry, has never evolved a national fish soup? It cannot be that the fish of northern waters are not suitable for soups and stews, for besides a large variety of molluscs and crustaceans which go so admirably into such dishes there are any number of white fish – skate, turbot, brill, bream, hake, halibut, haddock, plaice, to mention only the most obvious – which can make excellent soups. It is not, presumably, considering the way they are habitually served, out of consideration for the delicacy of their flavour that these fish are only steamed or fried. In any case, whatever the reason, there is a common notion in England that the only acceptable fish soup is a costly and troublesome lobster *bisque*. It seems to me that a study of Italian fish soups, of which there is a considerable variety, with ancient traditions, should have beneficial effects on our daily food.

Tomatoes, oil, onions, garlic, aromatic herbs, all the ingredients which go into a southern fish stew, we have. Obviously North Sea and Channel fish will produce a soup of different aspect and flavour from the *burrida* of Genoa, or the *brodetto* of the Adriatic, but, as we have no traditions to observe in these matters, this need cause no serious concern. Consider, for instance, the cheaper fish; the so-called rock salmon is good for a stew, as it does not disintegrate; those smoked or frozen cod fillets which are sometimes the only alternative in the fishmongers' to expensive sole or lobster respond better to a bath of aromatic tomato and lemon flavoured broth than to a blanket of flour and breadcrumbs . . . Why should cockles be confined to the pier at Southend, and soft roes to a slice of sodden toast, when these things are so cheap and make such a good basis for a fish stew? As for the vegetables, there is no need to restrict them, as the Italians do, to tomatoes and onions. Green peas and mushrooms, watercress and celery and cucumber, go admirably with fish. It is worth remembering that in the eighteenth century oranges were used as much for flavouring fish as are lemons today. Cider is not merely a substitute for white wine in cooking; the flavour it imparts to fish is excellent and original. People who like the taste of curry can use a scrap of curry paste or powder, or turmeric, in a fish stew instead of saffron; tarragon and fennel, mint and basil, nutmeg, mace, and coriander seeds (not all at once) are fine flavourings for fish. Garlic addicts will quickly perceive the charm of fried croûtons rubbed with garlic as an accompaniment to a fish broth. Here, then, in the devising of a really admirable English fish soup, is scope for inventiveness and imagination.

BURRIDA
Genoese Fish Stew

The fish the Genoese use for their *burrida* are the *scorfano* or *pesce cappone* (*scorpaena porcus*, the *rascasse* of the Provençal *bouillabaisse*); the *gallinella* (*trigla lyra*, sea-hen); the *pesce prete* (*uranoscopus scaber*, star-gazer); the *pescatrice* or *boldro* (*lophius piscatorius*, angler or frog-fish); eel or conger; the *scorfano rosso* (*scorpaena scrofa*, the *chapon* of Provence); octopus, inkfish, *nocciolo* or *palombo* (*mustelos laevis*, dogfish); *sugherello* (*trachurus*, a kind of mackerel). Clear outline drawings of all these fish, plus much other relevant information, are to be found in Alan Davidson's *Mediterranean Seafood* (Penguin).

To make the broth, heat about 2 oz. of olive oil in a wide saucepan. Put in a small chopped onion and let it brown slightly. Add half a carrot, a small piece of celery, a clove of garlic, and some parsley, all chopped small, and 2 or 3 anchovy fillets cut in pieces. After 5 minutes add 1 lb. of peeled and chopped tomatoes, or ¼ pint of freshly made tomato sauce, or a tablespoonful of tomato purée diluted with water, and ½ oz. of dried mushrooms which have been soaked a few minutes in water. Season with salt, pepper, and a little basil, and add a little water to the broth.

If octopus and inkfish are to be part of the *burrida* they should be put in while the broth is cooking and simmered a good 30 minutes. Now add a selection of the above-mentioned fish, cut into thick slices, and cook for about 20 minutes.

BRODETTO ALLA RAVENNATE
Ravenna Fish Soup

In the Marche and on the Adriatic coast fish soup is known as *brodetto*.

Several towns of the Adriatic coast, where the fish is

notably good, have their versions of *brodetto*; those of Ancona and Rimini are well known, and another good one comes from Ravenna Marina. It is worth while, when visiting Ravenna, to drive the five miles to the Marina and to eat *brodetto* a few yards from where the fish has been landed, in sight of the long stretch of white sand and the pine wood where Lord Byron used to ride. After luncheon, if it is a fine day, go down to the port to see the fishing boats coming in with the day's catch; their sails are a fine patchwork of Adriatic colours, bright clear blues, rose reds, chrome yellow, faded green, cobalt violet; the nets are dyed black, and slung between the masts to dry.

Here is the recipe for fish soup as it is made at Ravenna Marina. It must be left to the imagination and resourcefulness of the reader to devise something as good and beautiful with North Sea fish.

The fish to be used for the *brodetto* are two or three different varieties of squid (*seppie, calamaretti, calamaroni*), eel, red mullet, *spigola* (sea bass), sole, and *cannocchie* (*squilla mantis*), a flat-tailed Adriatic and Mediterranean crustacean with a delicate flavour and lilac marks on its white flesh. Also called *pannocchie* and *cicala di mare*.

First of all make the *brodo* or *sugo* (the broth, which is the basis of all Italian fish soups). Put the heads of the fish into a pan with parsley, pounded garlic, tomatoes, salt, pepper, *origano*, and a little vinegar. When the tomatoes and the fish are cooked, remove all the bones and sieve the broth. Keep aside this broth, which should be fairly thin and of a deep red-brown colour.

Into a wide shallow earthenware pan put some olive

oil and parsley and garlic pounded together. When the oil is hot add a fair quantity of sauce made from fresh tomatoes and thinned with a little water. Put in the prepared and cleaned *seppie*, for they must cook for a good 30 minutes before all the other fish, which are to be added, at the appropriate moment, cut into thick slices. Cook them gently and without stirring or they will break – 30 minutes should be sufficient.

Remove them from their sauce, which will be nearly all absorbed by this time. Arrange them in a hot dish. Heat up the prepared *brodo*, and in this put rounds of bread either fried in oil or baked in the oven.

The broth and the fish are handed round at the same time but in separate dishes, so that each person may help himself to the variety of fish he chooses.

It will be seen that, owing to the variety of fish required, it is pointless to attempt this soup for fewer than six or eight people.

ZUPPA DI PESCE ALLA ROMANA
Roman Fish Soup

The Romans are great eaters of fish soup; their recipes vary a good deal. Here is a particularly good one.

A *morena* (a kind of lamprey), a *pescatrice* (angler fish), *cappone* (the *rascasse* of the Provençal coast, a scaly fish of which there is no equivalent in northern waters), *scorfano* (much the same as the Provençal *chapon*; again, we have no such fish in England), inkfish, octopus, mussels, clams, *scampi*.

First of all boil the cleaned octopus and the inkfish.

Make a fish stock with the heads and tails of the white fish, celery, garlic, and parsley. Strain it when it is cooked.

In another pan sauté a chopped clove of garlic and a fillet or two of anchovy in olive oil, and to this add 1 lb. of peeled and chopped tomatoes and a little chopped parsley. After 5 minutes put in the white fish cut into slices and the already cooked octopus and inkfish; let them cook a little and add the shellfish, cleaned and scrubbed very carefully, in their shells. Now add the prepared stock, and as soon as the shellfish have opened the soup is ready.

Serve it in a tureen with fried bread.

A FISH STEW OR SOUP

2 fillets of lemon sole, ½ lb. of halibut, ½ lb. of smoked cod fillet, 2 oz. of shelled prawns.

For the broth: a small onion, ½ lb. of tomatoes, half a small cucumber, parsley, 2 oz. of olive oil, ¼ pint of water, mace, red and black pepper, bay leaves, thyme, 3 cloves of garlic, and a small glassful of white wine.

Heat the olive oil in a wide pan; melt the sliced onion; add the cloves of garlic, the chopped parsley, the cucumber unpeeled and cut into small dice, and the skinned and chopped tomatoes. Season with salt, the red and black pepper, and a little mace. Add the white wine, then the water. Simmer for 20 minutes. If the broth is too thick add a little water.

Cut the fish into thick slices, removing the skin if possible. Put the smoked cod first into the broth, and

5 minutes later the halibut; then the lemon sole, adding the prawns only for 2 or 3 minutes at the end of the cooking.

If you have some inkfish preserved in oil, add a few slices at the same time as the halibut; a pint of mussels in their shells is another alternative. Cut a little fresh parsley over the soup before it is served.

Have ready 4 slices of a French loaf for each person, baked golden in a slow oven and afterwards rubbed with a piece of cut garlic. Put this prepared bread into each soup plate before serving.

Enough for three or four people.

One needs a fork for the solids, as well as a spoon for the broth.

A LAST WORD ABOUT FISH SOUPS

Let those who cannot abide fish soups and detest extracting fish-bones from their mouths take heart. They are not alone. For their benefit I quote what Norman Douglas had to say about *zuppa di pesce* when he wrote *Siren Land* in 1911 (it is true that a badly made fish soup is perfectly detestable, and it cannot be claimed that the cooking in Naples and roundabout is always very *soigné*. This does not alter my personal opinion that a *good* fish soup is lovely food). For the rest, Norman Douglas's triumphant warnings of the appalling fate which would certainly overtake anyone so foolhardy as to eat mussels, *aguglie*, *palombo* ('of course, if you *care* to eat shark, my dear') were repeated mainly to disconcert; he was himself the first to mock at the absurdity of food fads.

'We have a fish soup; *guarracini* and *scorfani* and *aguglie* and *toteri* and . . .

'Take breath, gentle maiden, the while I explain to the patient reader the ingredients of the diabolical preparation known as *zuppa di pesce*. The *guarracino*, for instance, is a pitch-black marine monstrosity, 1–2 in. long, a mere blot, with an Old Red Sandstone profile and insufferable manners, whose sole recommendation is that its name is derived from *koraxinos*. (*Korax* . . . a raven; but who can live on Greek roots?) As to the *scorfano*, its name is unquestionably onomatopœic, to suggest the spitting-out of bones; the only difference, from a culinary point of view, between the *scorfano* and a toad being that the latter has twice as much meat on it. The *aguglia*, again, is all tail and proboscis; the very nightmare of a fish – as thin as a lead pencil. Who would believe that for this miserable sea-worm with verdigris-tinted spine, which an ordinary person would thank you for not setting on his table, the inhabitants of Siren land fought like fiends? The blood of their noblest was shed in defence of privileges artfully wheedled out of Anjou and Aragonese kings defining the *ius quoddam pescandi vulgariter dictum sopra le aguglie*; that a certain tract of sea was known as the "aguglie water" and owned, up to the days of Murat, by a single family who defended it with guns and man-traps? And everybody knows the *totero* or squid, an animated ink-bag of perverse leanings, which swims backwards because all other creatures go forwards and whose india-rubber flesh might be useful for deluding hunger on desert islands, since, like American gum, you can chew it for months but never get it down.

'These, and such as they, float about in a lukewarm brew of rancid oil and garlic, together with a few of last week's breadcrusts, decaying sea-shells and onion peels, to give it an air of consistency.

'This is the stuff for which Neapolitans sell their female relatives. But copious libations will do wonders with a *zuppa di pesce*.

' "Wine of Marciano, signore."

' "Then it must be good. It grows on the mineral."

' "Ah, you foreigners know everything."

'We do; we know, for example, that nothing short of a new creation of the world will ever put an end to that legend about the mineral.

'How unfavourably this hotch-potch compares with the Marseillese *bouillabaisse*! But what can be expected, considering its ingredients? Green and golden scales, and dorsal fins embellished with elaborate rococo designs, will satisfy neither a hungry man nor an epicure, and if Neapolitans pay untold sums for the showy Mediterranean seaspawn it only proves that they eat with their eyes, like children, who prefer tawdry sweets to good ones. They have colour and shape, these fish of the inland sea, but not taste. Their flesh is either flabby and slimy and full of bones in unauthorised places or else they have no flesh at all – heads like Burmese dragons but no bodies attached to them; or bodies of flattened construction on the *magnum in parvo* principle, allowing of barely room for a sheet of paper between their skin and ribs; or a finless serpentine framework, with long-slit eyes that leer at you while you endeavour to scratch a morsel off the reptilian anatomy.

'There is not a cod, or turbot, or whiting, or salmon, or herring in the two thousand miles between Gibraltar and Jerusalem; or if there is, it never comes out. Its haddocks (haddocks, indeed!) taste as if they had fed on mouldy sea-weed and died from the effects of it; its lobsters have no claws; its oysters are bearded like pards; and as for its soles – I have yet to see one that measures more than 5 in. round the waist. The fact is, there is hardly a fish in the Mediterranean worth eating, and therefore – *ex nihilo nihil fit. Bouillabaisse* is only good because cooked by the French, who, if they cared to try, could produce an excellent and nutritious substitute out of cigar-stumps and empty matchboxes. But even as a Turk is furious with a tender chicken because it cheats him out of the pleasure of masticating, so the Neapolitan would throw a boneless *zuppa di pesce* out of the window: the spitting and spluttering is half the fun.'

FRENCH DISHES

Summer Greenery

Between the fake luxury of the lavishly upholstered avocado (the development by the Israelis of a stoneless avocado shaped like a little fat sausage is going to spoil all the fun) and the chilly squalor of the slice of emulsified pâté perched on a lettuce leaf, what is there for the hors d'oeuvre course during our English summer months? No prizes. There is – apart from delicious English specialities like dressed fresh crab, Scottish smoked salmon and potted smoked haddock – a whole world of beautiful and delicate luxuries, true luxuries, such as fresh purple sprouting broccoli, fine French beans, asparagus, cooked and served almost before they have become cold, with a perfectly simple olive oil and lemon juice dressing. Above all, there are, less expensive than any of these delicacies, English-grown courgettes, the only truly new vegetable successfully produced in this country since the great tomato transplant of the turn of the century.

It is from Greece and the countries of the Eastern Mediterranean that Western Europe has learned how to appreciate this delicious and versatile miniature vegetable marrow. It was, curiously enough, in the island of Malta during the mid-thirties that I first became aware of the existence of the courgette. Locally grown, I fancy, on the island of Gozo, the courgettes were the smallest I have ever seen, no longer than a little finger. They were almost invariably cooked whole, unpeeled, and finished in a cheese-flavoured cream sauce. An excellent dish and one which for years I attempted to achieve at home, using courgettes far too big to be cooked whole. Nowadays I think that there are far better ways of eating the courgette. The Italians, the Egyptians, the Greeks, the southern French, all have first-class recipes. I could, but shall probably not, write a whole book about courgettes. At the moment I shall confine myself to three recipes which all in their different ways make appealing and fresh first-course dishes. (I cannot bring myself to use the terms appetiser or starter. The first is meaningless in the context, the second makes me think of a man on a racecourse with a stop-watch in his hand.)

The courgette dishes are all, I think, best served as suggested in the recipes rather than as part of a mixed hors d'oeuvre. They do not combine happily with pâtés or with crudités such as fennel, radishes, and the sweet pepper salad given further on in this article.

More positive suggestions are: a sliced hard-boiled egg or two to make up part of a mixed courgette salad; and it is worth knowing that fresh prawns – on a separate dish – make a first-class combination with courgettes.

For the rest, the vital points are the split-second timing of the boiling of vegetables to be served as salads; the importance of seasoning, when and what; the reminders that seventy-five per cent of the delicacy of most such salads is lost once they have spent so much as one hour under refrigeration and that they do not in any case keep very long, and should therefore be cooked in small quantities and quickly eaten; finally, that elegant presentation is one of the first considerations. Inviting appearance does create appetite. If a dish, any dish, is enticing enough to arouse appetite, then I would think it reasonable that it should be called an appetiser, no matter at what stage of the meal it is offered.

COURGETTES IN SALAD

Choose the smallest courgettes you can find. Allow 500 g (1 lb) for 4 people. Other ingredients are salt, water, olive oil, lemon juice or mild wine vinegar, parsley.

To prepare the courgettes for cooking, cut a small slice off each end. Wash the courgettes and, with a potato parer, pare off any rough or blemished strips of skin, so that the outside of the vegetable looks striped, pale and dark green.

Cut each courgette into about 4-cm (1½-in) lengths. Put them into an enamel-lined or flameproof porcelain saucepan. Cover them with cold water. Add 1 dessertspoon of salt. Bring the water to the boil, cover the pan, simmer for approximately 20 minutes. Test the courgettes with a skewer. (A kebab skewer, its point protected with a cork, is a working implement I find indispensable.) They should be tender but not mushy. Immediately they are cooked drain them in a colander.

Have ready a well-seasoned dressing made with fine olive oil and wine vinegar. In this, mix the courgettes while they are still warm. Arrange them in a shallow white salad bowl and scatter a little very finely chopped parsley over them before serving.

Freshly cooked beetroot, French beans, whole small peeled tomatoes and possibly flowerets of cauliflowers dressed in the same manner as the courgettes can be arranged to alternate, in small neat clumps (not mixed higgledy-piggledy), with the courgettes.

In the days of the British Protectorate in Egypt, a vegetable salad prepared in this fashion was a familiar dish on the tables of English and Anglo-Egyptian families and in the British clubs of Cairo, Alexandria and Port Said. Well prepared and with a good dressing, the cold vegetables make a delicate and refreshing salad to be eaten either as a first course or after a roast of meat or chicken. Great care should be taken not to overcook the courgettes or they will be waterlogged and no more interesting than nursery cabbage.

N.B. It should go without saying that since the size and the thickness of courgettes vary a good deal, the cooking time may also need a little adjustment.

SWEET GREEN PEPPER SALAD

The first time I tasted a sweet pepper salad made in the way described below was in an hotel at Orange, on the road south to Provence.

The spread of crudités brought to the table on an hors d'oeuvre tray looked, even in a part of the country where the hors d'oeuvres are always fresh and shining, especially appetising. There were the usual salads, tomato, cucumber, grated raw carrots, olives green and black, anchovies, and this salad of green peppers cut so finely that when we first saw them we thought they were shredded French beans. There is nothing in the least complicated about preparing it, but if it's to be made in any quantity it does take a little time.

For part of a mixed hors d'oeuvre for 3 or 4 people you need one large green sweet pepper, weighing about 200–250 g (7–8 oz), plus a small quantity of onion, salt, sugar, olive oil, vinegar, lemon juice, parsley.

Cut the stalk end from the pepper and discard all seeds and core. Rinse very thoroughly. Cut the pepper across into strips about 3.5 cm (1½ in) wide. Slice each of these strips into the thinnest possible little slivers, scarcely longer than a match. Put them into a bowl. Add a very little thinly sliced onion – no more than a tea-spoonful. Season rather generously with salt, add a pinch of sugar, then 3 tablespoons of olive oil, one of wine vin-egar, a squeeze of lemon juice, and a sprinkling of parsley. And, if possible, make the salad an hour or so in advance. Sweet peppers are all the better for being marinated in their dressing a little while before they are to be eaten.

Greek white cheese or feta is nearly always eaten as a meze or first course and goes uncommonly well with raw vegetables such as fennel, the shredded peppers described above, radishes, and with new broad beans. The latter are simply put on the table, as they are, in the pod, on a big dish. Sea salt and good coarse bread should be part of this primitive summer feast.

Tians

Among the very simplest and easiest of summer dishes
are those mixtures of vegetables and eggs baked in an
open earthenware casserole or gratin dish called in the
Provençal language a *tian*. From the earthenware *tian*,
the dish itself takes its name. Not that there is any one
specific formula for a *tian*; there are as many variations as there are of a *salade niçoise*, the idea being that
you use a certain proportion of freshly cooked green
vegetables – spinach, spinach beet or chard (the kind
the French call *blettes*) – bulking them out, if you like,
with potatoes or rice and mixing them all up with eggs
beaten as for an omelette. The proportions depend to a
certain extent upon what you have available, the size of
your dish, the number of people you have to feed. Seasonings and extra flavourings may be onions, garlic,
anchovies, capers. Grated cheese – usually Gruyère, Parmesan or Dutch – and plenty of chopped parsley and
other fresh green herbs are fairly constant ingredients.
Sometimes a richly aromatic tomato sauce goes into the
mixture. A *tian*, as you see, is a wonderfully flexible dish,
not the least of its beauties being that it is equally good
hot or cold; it is indeed a traditional picnic dish of the
country people around Arles, Avignon and Aix-en-
Provence. Every family has a different recipe. Some are
just simple mixtures of vegetables and cheese with a top

layer of breadcrumbs and without any eggs at all, although these I think are best eaten hot. My own favourites are made with courgettes, potatoes and eggs, or with spinach, potatoes and eggs.

TIAN OR GRATIN OF COURGETTES, TOMATOES AND EGGS

This is one version – entirely my own and a much simplified one – of the Provençal country dish called a *tian*.

Please do not be daunted by the length of the recipe which follows. Once this dish has been mastered – and it is not at all difficult – you find that you have learned at least three dishes as well as a new way of preparing and cooking courgettes.

The ingredients of my *tian* are: 500 g (1 lb) of courgettes, 750 g (1½ lb) of tomatoes (in England use 500 g (1 lb) of fresh tomatoes and make up the quantity with Italian tinned whole peeled tomatoes and their juice), 1 small onion, 2 cloves of garlic, fresh basil when in season, and in the winter dried French marjoram or tarragon, 4 large eggs, a handful (i.e. about 3 tablespoons) of grated Parmesan or Gruyère cheese, a handful of coarsely chopped parsley, salt, freshly milled pepper, nutmeg. For cooking the courgettes and tomatoes, a mixture of butter and olive oil.

The quantities given should be enough for 4 people but the proportions are deliberately somewhat vague because *tian* is essentially a dish to be made from the ingredients you have available. If, for instance, you have 250g (½lb) only of courgettes, make up the bulk with

4 tablespoons of cooked rice, or the same bulk in diced cooked potatoes.

To prepare the courgettes, wash them and pare off any parts of the skins which are blemished, leaving them otherwise unpeeled. Slice them lengthways into four, then cut them into 1-cm (½-in) chunks. Put them at once into a heavy frying pan or enamelled cast-iron skillet or gratin dish, sprinkle them with salt, and set them *without fat of any kind* over a very low flame. Watch them carefully, and when the juices, brought out by the salt, start to seep out, turn the courgettes with a spatula, and drop into the pan 30 g (1 oz) or so of butter, then a tablespoon or two of olive oil. Cover the pan, and leave the courgettes over a low heat to soften.

While the courgettes are cooking prepare the tomatoes. Pour boiling water over them, skin them, chop them roughly. Peel and chop the onion. Heat a very little butter or olive oil in an earthenware *poêlon* or whatever utensil you habitually use for making a tomato fondue or sauce. First melt the chopped onion without letting it brown. Then put in the tomatoes, season them, add the peeled and crushed garlic. Cook, uncovered, over low heat until a good deal of the moisture is evaporated. Now add the tinned tomatoes. These, and their juices, give colour, body and the necessary sweetness to the sauce. Sprinkle in the herb of your choice, let the tomato mixture cook until it is beginning to reduce and thicken.

Now amalgamate the courgettes and the tomato mixture. Turn them into a buttered or oiled earthenware gratin dish. For the quantities given, use one of approximately 18 cm (7 in) diameter and 5 cm (2 in) depth.

Put the gratin dish, covered with a plate if it has no lid of its own, in a moderate oven (170°C/325°F/gas mark 3) for about half an hour, until the courgettes are quite tender.

To finish the *tian*, beat the eggs very well with the cheese, add plenty of seasonings (don't forget the nutmeg) and the coarsely chopped parsley.

Amalgamate the eggs and the vegetable mixture, increase the heat of the oven to 180–190°C/350–375°F/gas mark 4 or 5, and leave the *tian* to cook until the eggs are set, risen in the dish, and beginning to turn golden on the top. The time varies between 15 and 25 minutes depending on various factors such as the depth of the dish, the comparative density of the vegetable mixture, the freshness of the eggs and so on.

When the *tian* is to be eaten cold, leave it to cool in its dish before inverting it on to a serving dish or plate. It should turn out into a very beautiful looking cake, well-risen and moist. For serving cut it in wedges. Inside, there will be a mosaic of pale green and creamy yellow, flecked with the darker green of the parsley and the red-gold of the tomatoes.

To transport a *tian* on a picnic, it can be left in its cooking dish, or turned out on to a serving plate. Whichever way you choose, cover the *tian* with greaseproof paper and another plate, then tie the whole arrangement in a clean white cloth, knotted Dick Whittington fashion.

TIAN WITH SPINACH AND POTATOES

Wash 500 g (1 lb) of fresh spinach, cook it very briefly in just the water clinging to the leaves. Season with a

little salt. Drain and squeeze dry. Chop it roughly, adding a little garlic if you like, and half a dozen anchovy
fillets torn into short lengths. Stir this mixture into the
beaten eggs and cheese, then add the cubed potatoes,
and cook the *tian* as before. If you can lay hands on a few
pine nuts, they make a delicious and characteristic addition to this *tian*. An alternative to the potatoes is cooked
rice. Allow about 100 g (3½ oz), uncooked weight, for
this size of *tian*.

Meat Dishes

SAUCE AU VIN DU MÉDOC
Beef, Rabbit and Pork or Hare Stewed in Red Wine

Here is a dish which is something of a collector's piece. I did not have to search for the recipe because I did not know of its existence. It fell, in a most felicitous way, into my outstretched hands through the kindness of Miss Patricia Green, a highly enterprising young woman who has made a study of wine and wine production on the spot in the Médoc.

From Madame Bernard, the wife of a wine-grower of Cissac-Médoc, Miss Green obtained this recipe and passed it on to me exactly as it was given to her; and she told me that Madame Bernard knew as much as there was to know of the peasant cooking of the region. I should also perhaps add that the name of the dish is not a printer's error, nor does it mean you throw away the meat and only eat the sauce; for, although the meat is cooked so slowly for so long that it practically is sauce, it is not uncommon in country districts of France to hear a stew of this kind referred to as la sauce.

Here is the recipe, unaltered in any particular. You may think it needs an act of faith to try it but when you read the recipe carefully you see that it is not really so strange and wild as it seems at a first glance.

1 rabbit, 1½ lb. stewing beef, 1 hare or 1½ lb. lean pork, 6 shallots, 4 cloves of garlic, 1 bayleaf, small sprig of thyme, large bundle of parsley, 1 dessertspoon of flour, salt, sugar, 1 square of plain chocolate, 1 bottle red wine, equal quantity of water, 3 large carrots, pork dripping or oil.

This is essentially a peasant dish, '*la grosse cuisine de la campagne*', and it should therefore be as rich and vulgarly hearty a savoury stew as possible when finished. It will be spoilt if the meat is cut into too delicate pieces or the carrots carefully sliced.

Heat the oil or, better still, pork dripping, in a large, thick saucepan which has a closely fitting lid. Cut the shallots very finely, and slowly and gently brown them in the hot fat, adding the carrots carefully peeled but cut only in 2 or 3 pieces. Sprinkle generously with salt, and when well browned add the meat. For pork and beef, trim off gristle and excess fat and cut into rather large chunks. For hare and rabbit, dry the joints well before adding to the frying vegetables. Brown the meat well all over, then add the garlic finely sliced, and the herbs, sprinkle with flour and mix all well together. Now pour on a bottle of red wine and bring quickly to the boil and bubble vigorously for about 5 minutes, reduce the heat, add an equal quantity of water, stir well, add a teaspoon of sugar and 1 small square of plain chocolate. Put on the lid and simmer, just a murmur, for about 3 hours. Allow to get quite cold. On the second day simmer again for about 2 hours before serving. Taste before doing so and adjust seasoning; it may be a little sharp, in which case a sprinkle more sugar will usually put matters right.

The choice of meats, as you see, is left pretty well to individual taste (shin of beef cut from the bone and sparerib or hand of pork *on* the bone with its skin is what I use, plus a hare or rabbit if either happen to be available). A whole bottle of wine and an equal quantity of water seems a lot of liquid, and this question is one which frequently arises in French recipes of this type, because the French peasants and workmen reckon on filling out their meal with a great deal of bread soaked in the sauce; in fact, two-thirds of the quantities can be used, but less I think would deprive the dish of its character.

As for the chocolate, of which rather less than an ounce is needed, it is not an uncommon ingredient in Italian and Spanish cookery, particularly in hare dishes, and is there as a sweetening and thickening for the sauce. Its use perhaps filtered down to the Bordelais through the channel of Basque and Béarnais cookery. And Bayonne, for generations one of the great chocolate manufacturing centres of France, is not far off.

CASSOULET DE TOULOUSE
À LA MÉNAGÈRE
Beans with Pork, Lamb and Sausages

To cook the better known version of the cassoulet, in quantities for about eight to ten people, the ingredients would be 2 lb. of medium-sized white haricot beans (butter beans will not do), 1 lb. of Toulouse sausages (a coarse-cut type of pure-pork sausage to be bought at Soho shops) or a garlic-flavoured boiling sausage of the kind now sold by most delicatessen shops, a pork sparerib or bladebone weighing about 2½ lb., 1½ lb. breast or shoulder of lamb (both joints boned), 8 to 10 oz. of salt pork or green bacon, an onion, a bouquet of herbs, garlic and seasonings, breadcrumbs.

Have the rind of the pork removed as thinly as possible. Remove also the rind from the salt pork. Cut these rinds into small squares and put them into the saucepan with the salt pork and beans, previously soaked. Add the onion and the bouquet of herbs, plus 2 flattened cloves of garlic, all tied with a thread. Cover with water and boil steadily for about 1½ hours. In the meantime roast the pork and the boned lamb in a gentle oven. If Toulouse sausages are being used, cook them for 20 minutes in the baking dish with the meat. If a boiling sausage, cook it with the beans.

When the beans are all but cooked, drain them, reserving their liquid. Discard the onion and the bouquet. Put a layer of the beans, with all the little bits of rind, into a deep earthenware or fireproof china dish; on the top put the sausages cut into inch lengths, and the lamb and the two kinds of pork, also cut into pieces. Cover with the rest of the beans. Moisten with a good cupful of the reserved liquid. Spread a layer of breadcrumbs on the top. Put in a very low oven for 1½ hours at least. There should be a fine golden crust on the top formed by the breadcrumbs, and underneath the beans should be very moist and creamy. So if you see during the second cooking that they are beginning to look dry, add some more liquid. Some cooks elaborate on this by stirring the crust, as soon as it has formed, into the beans, then adding another layer of breadcrumbs. This operation is repeated a second time, and only when the third crust has formed is the cassoulet ready to serve.

The cassoulet is a dish which may be infinitely varied so long as it is not made into a mockery with a sausage or two heated up with tinned beans, or with all sorts of bits of left-over chicken or goodness knows what thrown into it as if it were a dustbin. And the wise will heed M. Colombié's advice about eating the cassoulet at midday on a day when no great exertion is called for afterwards.

If you are visiting Toulouse, a lovely cassoulet is to be had at the Restaurant Richelieu-Michel in the rue Gabriel-Péri, but probably it will not be on the menu during the hot summer months.

LA DAUBE DE BŒUF PROVENÇALE
Provençal Meat and Wine Stew

There must be scores of different recipes for daubes in Provence alone, as well as all those which have been borrowed from Provence by other regions, for a daube of beef is essentially a country housewife's dish. In some daubes the meat is cut up, in others it is cooked in the piece; what goes in apart from the meat is largely a matter of what is available, and the way it is served is again a question of local taste.

This is an easy recipe, but it has all the rich savour of these slowly cooked wine-flavoured stews. The pot to cook it in may be earthenware, cast iron, or a copper or aluminium oven pot of about 2 pints capacity, wide rather than deep.

The ingredients are 2 lb. of top rump of beef, about 6 oz. of unsmoked streaky bacon or salt pork, about 3 oz.

of fresh pork rinds, 2 onions, 2 carrots, 2 tomatoes, 2 cloves of garlic, a bouquet of thyme, bayleaf, parsley and a little strip of orange peel, 2 tablespoons of olive oil, a glass (4 fl. oz.) of red wine, seasoning.

Have the meat cut into squares about the size of half a postcard and about 1/3 inch thick. Buy the bacon or salt pork in the piece and cut it into small cubes.

Scrape and slice the carrots on the cross; peel and slice the onions. Cut the rinds, which should have scarcely any fat adhering to them and are there to give body as well as savour to the stew, into little squares. Skin and slice the tomatoes.

In the bottom of the pot put the olive oil, then the bacon, then the vegetables and half the pork rinds. Arrange the meat carefully on top, the slices overlapping each other. Bury the garlic cloves, flattened with a knife, and the bouquet, in the centre. Cover with the rest of the pork rinds. With the pan uncovered, start the cooking on a moderate heat on top of the stove.

After about 10 minutes, put the wine into another sauce-pan; bring it to a fast boil; set light to it; rotate the pan so that the flames spread. When they have died down pour the wine bubbling over the meat. Cover the pot with grease-proof paper or foil, and a well-fitting lid. Transfer to a very slow oven, Gas No. 1, 290 deg. F., and leave for 2½ hours.

To serve, arrange the meat with the bacon and the little pieces of rind on a hot dish; pour off some of the fat from the sauce, extract the bouquet, and pour the sauce round the meat. If you can, keep the dish hot over a spirit lamp after it is brought to table. At the serving stage, a *persillade* of finely chopped garlic and parsley, with perhaps an anchovy and a few capers, can be sprinkled over the top. Or stoned black olives can be added to the stew half an hour before the end of the cooking time.

Although in Italy pasta is never served with a meat dish, in Provence it quite often is. The cooked and drained noodles, or whatever pasta you have chosen, are mixed with some of the gravy from the stew, and in this case the fat is not removed from the gravy, because it lubricates the pasta. Sometimes this *macaronade*, as it is called, is served first, to be followed by the meat.

Nowadays, since rice has been successfully cultivated in the reclaimed areas of the Camargue, it is also quite usual to find a dish of rice, often flavoured with saffron, served with a meat stew.

This daube is a useful dish for those who have to get a dinner ready when they get home from the office. It can be cooked for 1½ hours the previous evening and finished on the night itself. Provided they have not been overcooked to start with, these beef and wine stews are all the better for a second or even third heating up. The amounts I have given are the smallest quantities in which it is worth cooking such a stew, and will serve four or five people, but of course they can be doubled or even trebled for a large party; if the meat is piled up in layers in a deep pan it will naturally need longer cooking than if it is spread out in a shallow one.

Christmas in France

Dinner on Christmas Eve in a French farmhouse of the pre-1914 era was a succession of homely country dishes for which almost every ingredient would have been produced on the farm itself. A characteristic menu, sustaining and solid, reads as follows:

Poule au riz à la fermière

Jambon cuit au foin

Petits pois jaunes en purée

Dindonneaux farcis aux marrons

Salade de céleris et betteraves

Poires étuvées au vin rouge

Galettes à la boulangère

Fromage de la ferme

Café. Vieux Marc

Vins: Moulin-à-Vent et . . . eau de puits

Escoffier, recording the dinner in a professional culinary magazine in the year 1912, thought it, in its 'rustic simplicity', worthy of inclusion among the festive menus of the Majestics, the Palaces, the Ritz-Carltons. the Excelsiors of Europe. How many of these menus, he asks, would be in such perfect taste? One senses a hint of envy in his words, for any chef who served such a menu in an English restaurant of the period would have been a laughing stock. The Carlton (where Escoffier was then presiding) Christmas menu for that year started with the inevitable caviare and turtle soup, and went on through the fillets of sole with crayfish sauce, the quails and stuffed lettuces, lamb cutlets, out-of-season asparagus, the foie gras and frosted tangerines, to start again with the truffled turkey, celery salad, plum pudding, hothouse peaches, *friandises*. At an elegant Paris restaurant, the Marguery, the Christmas Eve dinner at the same period consisted of one service only. Oysters, consommé with poached eggs, timbale of lobster, truffled chicken or pheasant, green salad, pâté de foie gras (in those days served after the roast rather than as an hors-d'oeuvre), an ice, plum pudding or *bûche de Noël*, fruit. The only concession to the festive season is the inclusion of the plum pudding and Yule log, otherwise it might have been a well chosen dinner for any winter's evening. For Christmas in France has never been quite the occasion for the prodigious feasts of the Germanic and Anglo-Saxon countries. A people for whom food is one of the first considerations every day of the year tend to regard the English preoccupation with eating for one week only out of the fifty-two, as rather gross.

Alfred Suzanne, whose book on *La Cuisine Anglaise* (he had been chef to the Duke of Bedford and the Earl of Wilton) is still the chief source of information to the

French about English cooking, referred to the 'hecatombs of turkeys, geese, game of all sorts, the holocaust of fatted oxen, pigs and sheep . . . mountains of plum puddings, ovens full of mince-pies'. Philéas Gilbert, another well known contemporary chef, went to some trouble to prove that '*le plum pudding n'est pas anglais*', but graciously conceded that, being already so rich in national dishes, the French could afford to leave the English in possession of their national Christmas pudding.

In most French country households the *réveillon* supper, however elegant the rest of the food, includes ritual dishes of humble origin such as boudins or blood puddings in some form or other, and various kinds of bread, biscuits, and galettes to which some ancient religious significance is attached. In Provence no fewer than thirteen of these desserts are traditional, while the main course is always a fish dish, usually salt cod, accompanied by snails, potatoes and other vegetables, salads and big bowls of the shining golden aïoli for which the finest olive oil has been reserved. For here the Christmas Eve supper is eaten before the celebration of Midnight Mass, and is therefore a *maigre* meal, shared by all the family, attended by the ceremony of sprinkling the Yule log with wine before setting it upon the fire, and the pronouncement, by the master of the house, of the prayer 'May God grant us grace to see the next year, and if there should not be more of us, let there not be fewer.'

When, as in Gascony and parts of the Languedoc, the ritual Christmas dish is one of those beef and wine *estoufats* which has been giving out its aromatic scents from the hearth where it has been simmering all day long, it will probably be eaten at one o'clock in the morning after the family comes back from Mass. The recipe for one such dish, from the Albi district, is so beautifully simple that its possibilities during the days of busy preparations for the festivities will be readily appreciated. For the rest, French turkeys, geese, hams and chickens are cooked much like our own, although the stuffings may vary, and the accompaniments are very much simpler – potatoes and a salad, a purée of dried split peas or a dish of rice, rather than the sprouts, the peas, the bread sauces, the gravies and sweet jellies of the English Christmas table.

ENGLISH DISHES

Toast

'No bread. Then bring me some toast!'

Punch, 1852

'"Toast," said Berry, taking the two last pieces that stood in the rack. "I'm glad to get back to toast. And a loaf of brown bread that isn't like potter's clay."'

Dornford Yates, *Adèle & Co.*, Ward, Lock, 1931

It isn't only fictional heroes to whom toast means home and comfort. It is related of the Duke of Wellington – I believe by Lord Ellesmere – that when he landed at Dover in 1814, after six years' absence from England, the first order he gave at the Ship Inn was for an unlimited supply of buttered toast.

In *The Origin of Food Habits* (1944), H. D. Renner makes an attempt to explain the English addiction to toast. 'The flavour of bread', he says, 'can be revived to some extent by re-warming and even new flavours are created in toasting.' This is very true, but leaves the most important part unsaid. It is surely the *smell* of toast that makes it so enticing, an enticement which the actuality rarely lives up to. In this it is like freshly roasted coffee, like sizzling bacon – all those early morning smells of an intensity and deliciousness which create far more than those new flavours, since they create hunger and appetite where none existed. Small wonder that the promise is never quite fulfilled. 'Village life', Renner continues, 'makes stale bread so common that toasting has become a national habit restricted to the British Isles and those countries which have been colonized by Britain.' Surely England was not the only country where villages were isolated and bread went dry and stale? I wonder if our open fires and coal ranges were not more responsible than the high incidence of stale bread for the popularity of toast in all classes of English household. For toasting bread in front of the fire and the bars of the coal-burning range there were dozens of different devices – museums of domestic life are crammed with them, Victorian cookery books show any number of designs – as many as there are varieties of electric toaster in our own day; apart from toasters for bread, there were special racks for toasting muffins and crumpets, and special pans for toasting cheese. And there were, in the nineteenth century, eminent medical men writing grave advice as to the kind of bread which, when toasted, would absorb the maximum amount of butter. That buttered toast goes back a long way in English life, and was by no means confined to country places where fresh bread was a rarity, is shown by the following quotation: 'All within the sound of Bow Bell', wrote Fynes Morison in *Itinerary*, Volume 3 (1617), 'are in reproch called cochnies, and eaters of buttered tostes.'

Buttered toast is, then, or was, so peculiarly English a delicacy – and I use the term delicacy because that is what in our collective national memory it still is – that the following meticulous description of how it was made, at least in theory, reads poignantly indeed. It is from the

86

hand of Miss Marian McNeill, author of that famous work *The Scots Kitchen*, on this occasion writing in an enchanting volume, long out of print,* called *The Book of Breakfasts*, published in 1932:

'Sweet light bread only a day old makes the best toast. Cut into even slices about quarter of an inch thick. It may be toasted under the grill, but the best toast is made at a bright smokeless fire. Put the slice on a toasting-fork and keep only so near the fire that it will be heated through when both sides are well browned. Move the toast about so as to brown evenly. Covered with an earthen bowl, toast will keep warm and moist.

'If very thin, crisp toast is desired, take bread that is two days old, cut it into slices about three-eighths of an inch thick, and toast them patiently at a little distance from a clear fire till delicately browned on both sides. With a sharp knife divide each slice into two thin slices, and toast the inner sides as before. Put each slice as it is done into a toast rack.

'For hot buttered toast, toast the bread more quickly than for ordinary toast, as it should not be crisp. Trim off the crusts and spread the toast liberally with butter that has been warmed but not allowed to oil. Cut in neat pieces, pile sandwichwise, and keep hot in a covered dish over a bowl of hot water. Use the best butter.'

I have my own childhood memories of toast-making in front of the schoolroom fire. Although I fancy that more toast fell off the fork into the fire and was irretrievably

* Since writing the above, *The Book of Breakfasts* has been reprinted by Reprographia (Edinburgh, 1975).

blackened than ever reached our plates, I can recall the great sense of achievement when now and again a slice did come out right, evenly golden, with a delicious smell and especially, as I remember, with the right, proper texture, so difficult to describe, and so fleeting. Only when it was hot from the fire and straight off the fork did that toast have the requisite qualities. Perhaps young children are better qualified than grown-ups to appreciate these points. And perhaps that is why buttered toast is one of those foods, like sausages, and potatoes baked in their skins, and mushrooms picked from the fields, which are never as good as they were.

Nowadays my toast is usually made on one of those ridged metal plates which goes over a gas flame or an electric burner. This produces crisp toast, very different from the kind made in front of the fire, but in its way almost as good. These lightweight metal toasters are very cheap. There is no need to buy an expensive iron one. Rye bread or 100 per cent whole wheatmeal bread both make excellent toast, but for buttered toast a light white bread is best. I prefer to make this kind of toast under the grill, electric toasters being machines with which I cannot be doing. In this I must be in a very small minority, for electric toasters are one of the most popular of all wedding presents, and in May 1975 *Which?* published a report on no fewer than thirteen different electric toasters. 'Some like it well done,' declared *Which?*, 'others pale brown; some like it done slowly to give a crisp finish, others done quickly so it's still soft inside.' All of these pronouncements are no doubt correct, as indeed is the statement that 'you don't want your piece of toast to be black in the middle and white round the edges'. That is to say, I don't. But I know plenty of people who actually *like* their toast to be charred. Perhaps they prefer it charred at the edges and white in the middle, and I'm not sure how this would be achieved. Another of the report's dictums, 'however you like your toast, you want all pieces to be more or less the same', is one I don't agree with, perhaps fortunately, for it is not easy to get all your pieces more or less the same. Unless, that is, you have a caterers' toasting machine and caterers' sliced bread which between them produce what I call restaurateurs' toast, that strange substance cut in triangles and served with the pâté, and for breakfast, in all English hotels and restaurants. This English invention has in recent years become popular in France where, oddly enough, it goes by the name of toast, as opposed to real French toast which is called *pain grillé*, and is just what it says, grilled bread. That brings me back to the toast-making device I myself use, the metal plate or grill over the gas burner. Part of the charm of the toast produced on this device is that every piece is different, and differently marked, irregularly chequered with the marks of the grill, charred here and there, flecked with brown and gold and black . . . I think that the goodness of toast made in this way does depend a good deal on the initial quality of the bread, and the way it is cut. Thin slices are useless, and I don't think that white sliced bread would be very successful – there is too much water to get rid of before the toasting process starts, and steamy bread sticks to the toaster. Thickish slices are best, preferably rather small ones which can be easily turned with grill tongs. Like most other toast, this kind is best straight from the grill. 'If allowed to stand and become sodden, dry toast becomes indigestible. From the fire to the table is the thing', wrote the delightfully named Lizzie Heritage in *Cassell's Universal Cookery Book* (first published 1894). And if the toast is to be buttered, I suppose we must remember Marian McNeill's 'use the best butter'. What *is* the best butter? Unsalted, some would say. I'll settle for any butter that's good of its kind. The very salt butter of Wales can be perfectly delicious eaten with the right kind of toast (no marmalade for me), and here is Flora Thompson* describing toast with salt butter and celery, and toast with cold boiled bacon. Toast-resistant though I am, she makes me long for that fresh hot toast and crisp celery, a wonderful combination, and how subtle:

'In winter, salt butter would be sent for and toast would be made and eaten with celery. Toast was a favourite dish for family consumption. "I've made 'em a stack o' toast as high as up to their knees", a mother would say on a winter Sunday afternoon before her hungry brood came in from church. Another dish upon which they prided themselves was thin slices of cold, boiled streaky bacon on toast, a dish so delicious that it deserves to be more widely popular.'

TOAST MELBA

'I remember one of those afternoons, at tea-time, I complained about the toast in Escoffier's hearing. "Toast is never thin enough to suit me," I said. "Can't you do

* *Lark Rise to Candleford*, 1945.

something about it?"

'As usual Escoffier and Ritz took such a remark with absolute seriousness. They discussed the problem of thin toast. "Why not," said Ritz, "toast thin slices of bread once, then cut it through again, and again toast it?" And with Escoffier he retired to the kitchens to see if it could not be done. The result was Escoffier's justly famous *toast Melba*. When they brought out on the lawn a plate full of the thin, crisp, curled wafers, Escoffier said, "Behold! A new dish, and it is called *toast Marie*." But as I ate it I tried to think up another name. Marie was far too anonymous to suit me.

'During that year Melba had returned from America very ill. She was staying at the Savoy where she was a much-indulged invalid. I had heard Escoffier discuss her *régime*. Dry toast figured on it . . . "Call it *toast Melba*," I said.

'And so it was done. I was the first to taste *toast Melba;* Madame Melba herself had to wait until the following day!'

Marie Ritz, *César Ritz. Host to the World*, 1938

You may or may not care for Melba toast, but there is something wonderfully pleasing in the picture evoked by Madame Ritz of the most celebrated chef and the most brilliant hotelier in all Europe getting together to make a few slices of thin toast and the result ending up with the name of a world-famous prima donna on a diet.

And was it then the alliance Escoffier–Ritz–Melba which was initially responsible for the idea of that restaurateurs' toast which subsequently became such a plague? Somewhere along the line things seem to have got a bit muddled. In the first place, Escoffier surely did not invent, nor claim to have invented, the method of slicing a piece of toast in half and then toasting the untoasted sides – see Marian McNeill's recipe quoted above – and the next awkward point is that Melba toast nowadays is usually understood to consist of thin, thin slices of bread toasted or rather dried in the oven until they curl round. Certainly it's a much easier and rather more successful method than all that slicing business.

PULLED BREAD

In the eighteenth and early nineteenth centuries 'pulling' bread was a fashionable way of producing crisp and crunchy pieces of bread to be eaten with cheese. The crumb of a newly baked loaf was torn into rough lumps, put back into the oven, and left until all the pieces were beginning to crisp on the outside but were still soft within. In effect, this was a form of toast.

I am not very seriously suggesting that anyone should bake a loaf especially to make pulled bread. There are times though when it may be a saving grace to know about pulled bread. For example, suppose that you have baked a loaf which turns out to be undercooked in the centre. Then you tear the crumb into pieces, put these pieces on a baking sheet or earthenware platter, and let them bake in a medium hot oven for about 10 to 15 minutes, until they are golden-flecked or pale toast coloured. They look and smell appetizing and fresh, and because they are not uniform each piece has a slightly different texture and its own character. They are really delicious and, I think, much more interesting than toast. It is worth trying pulled bread with pâté. It's quite a revelation.

To be good, pulled bread must be sufficiently salted; and it must have good texture and a little scrunchy bite. Soft baps and muffin loaves make good pulled bread.

According to Mr John Scade, author of a chapter on the local traditions of English breads, the names and shapes of loaves, and the different varieties of tea cakes, baps and buns, contributed to Ronald Sheppard and Edward Newton's *The Story of Bread* (1957), pulled bread is or was at that time still served 'at dinners and banquets from shallow napkin-covered baskets'.

Potted Meats and Fish

In the late forties and the early fifties, every new member of the Wine and Food Society received, together with a copy of the current number of the Society's quarterly magazine and a membership card, a pamphlet entitled *Pottery*, or *Home Made Potted Foods, Meat and Fish Pastes, Savoury Butters and Others*. The little booklet was a Wine and Food Society publication, the author's name was concealed under the whimsical pseudonym of 'A Potter', and the date was 1946.

The Wine and Food Society's propaganda in favour of homemade potted meats and fish was premature. In those days of rationing and imitation food we associated fish paste and potted meat with the fearful compounds of soya bean flour, dried egg and dehydrated onions bashed up with snoek or Spam which were cheerfully known as 'mock crab paste' and 'meat spread'. By 1954, when fourteen years of rationing came to an end none of us wanted to hear another word of the makeshift cooking which potted meats and fish pastes seemed to imply.

It was not until ten years later that we began to see that in fact these very English store-cupboard provisions, so far from being suited to the cheese-paring methods necessitated by desperate shortages, demand first-class basic ingredients and a liberal hand with butter. It is indeed essential to understand that the whole

94

success of the recipes described in this booklet depends upon these factors, and upon the correct balance of the ingredients.

Hungry as we are today for the luxury of authenticity and for visual elegance, we find that the Potter's work makes enticing reading: 'How delicious to a schoolboy's healthy appetite sixty years ago, was a potted meat at breakfast in my grandmother's old Wiltshire home. Neat little white pots, with a crust of yellow butter suggesting the spicy treat beneath, beef, ham or tongue, handiwork of the second or third kitchenmaid . . .'

The Potter whose grandmother employed the second and third kitchenmaids in question was, M. André Simon tells me, Major Matthew Connolly (father of Mr Cyril Connolly); and with his felicitous evocation of a mid-Victorian country breakfast table and those second and third kitchenmaids pounding away at the ham and tongue for potting he makes a number of points, most relevant of which concerns the kitchenmaids. What but the return of these handmaidens to our kitchens in the re-incarnated form of electric mixers, blenders and beaters* has made the revival of one of our most characteristic national delicacies a feasible proposition? Then, the neat little white pots, the crust of yellow butter, there is something fundamentally and uniquely English in the

---

* Of these machines by far the most effective for potted meats, as also for raw pâté ingredients, is the recently introduced French Moulinette Automatic Chopper. This device does the job of chopping and pounding without emulsifying the ingredients or squeezing out their juices.

picture evoked by Major Connolly. It is a picture which belongs as much to the world of Beatrix Potter (Major Connolly would no doubt have appreciated the coincidental pun) as to that of the military gentleman from Bath, making it doubly an insult that the mass-produced pastes and sandwich spreads of the factories should go by the honourable names of potted meat, potted ham, tongue, lobster, salmon, shrimp and the rest. Potted shrimps alone remain as the sole representative of these products to retain something of its original nature, although a few smoked haddock pastes are beginning to appear on London restaurant menus. These are usually somewhat absurdly listed as haddock pâté, or pâté de haddock fumé. In an expensive Chelsea restaurant I have even seen – and eaten – a mixture called *rillettes écossaises* or 'pâté of Arbroath smokies with whisky'. The dish was good, but to label such a mixture *rillettes* when this is a word applicable exclusively to potted fat pork, or pork with goose or rabbit, does seem to touch the fringe of restaurateur's lunacy. For that matter, I find it sad that Arbroath smokies, the most delicate, expensive and rare of all the smoked haddock tribe, should be subjected to such treatment. Simply heated through in the oven with fresh butter, smokies are to me one of the most exquisite of our national specialities.

That crust of yellow butter so important to the true English potted meats and pastes as opposed to the Franglais and the factory-produced versions, does perhaps need a little more explanation than the late Major Connolly, who refers to it throughout his little work as 'melted butter', thought necessary to clarify. Clarified in fact is what it is, or should be, that butter. And since for the successful confection and storage of many, although not all, potted meats and fish, clarified butter is a necessary adjunct, it seems only fair to warn readers that the process does involve a little bother, although a trifling one compared to the services rendered by a supply of this highly satisfactory sealing, mixing, and incidentally, frying ingredient.

STORAGE OF POTTED FOODS

Concerning the keeping qualities of home-potted foods, there are some essential points to make. First, all juices and liquid which come from fish or meat to be potted, whether especially cooked for the purpose or whether left-over from a joint, *must be drained off before the food is pounded or packed up for potting*. Because stock or gravy from salmon, game or beef, let us say, happens to look rich and taste delicious, that does not mean it will not go bad if it separates from the meat or fish in question and settles to the bottom of the pot. We all know what happens when jellied gravy and sediment is left at the bottom of a bowl of dripping or lard.

It is also important to eliminate as far as possible any air pockets in pots of meat and fish. This means that the pots must be packed very full and the contents pressed and pressed until they are as tightly packed as possible.

Finally, make sure that the layer of melted clarified butter with which the pots are covered is sufficiently thick to seal the contents completely. Given these conditions there is no reason why potted meat and fish should not keep, in a correctly ventilated larder, for several weeks. 'Game to be sent to distant places', wrote Meg Dods, long before the advent of the refrigerator, 'and potted without cutting up the birds will keep for a month.' Once broached, the contents of a pot should be stored in the refrigerator and quickly consumed. For this reason, potted meats and fish are essentially delicacies to be packed into small pots. Failing the old-fashioned neat white pots described by Major Connolly use miniature white china soufflé dishes or ramekins, small straight-sided glass jars, foie gras or pâté terrines, or white, covered pots such as those associated with Gentleman's Relish – still a favourite fish paste. Apart from the dimensions and shape of the pot, an important point to remember is that whatever the colour or decoration on the *outside* of the pots or jars used for potted meats, the *inside* should be of a pale colour and preferably white, so that the delicate creams and pinks of the contents with their layer of yellow butter look fresh and appetizing against their background.

WHEN AND HOW TO SERVE POTTED FOODS AND PASTES

'A noble breakfast,' says George Borrow of the morning meal offered him at an inn at Bala in North Wales, 'there was tea and coffee, a goodly white loaf and butter, there were a couple of eggs and two mutton chops – there was boiled and pickled salmon – fried trout . . . also potted trout and potted shrimps . . .' A few weeks later he returns in search of more country delicacies. He is not disappointed. 'What a breakfast! Pot of hare; ditto of trout; pot of prepared shrimps; dish of plain shrimps; tin of sardines; beautiful beef-steak; eggs, muffins, large loaf, and butter, not forgetting capital tea . .'

George Borrow was writing of *Wild Wales* in the eighteen-fifties. When you come to analyse his splendid breakfasts you find that with slight changes he might almost be describing a nineteen-sixties, chop-house revival period, West End restaurant lunch. The potted shrimps, the trout, the steak, the pot of hare (now the chef's *terrine de lièvre*), the mutton chops (now lamb cutlets), the salmon, now smoked rather than pickled, are very much with us still. The March of Progress has alas transformed the goodly white bread into that unique substance, restaurateurs' toast, while tea and coffee are replaced by gin-and-tonic or a bottle of white wine, and for my part I would say none the worse for that. Tea with a fish breakfast or coffee with beefsteaks have never been my own great favourites in the game of what to drink with what.

Here we are then with plenty of ideas for an easy and simple English lunch; potted tongue or game followed by a simple hot egg dish; or smoked salmon paste with butter and brown bread to precede grilled lamb chops, or oven-baked sole, or fillet steak if you are rich. For a high-tea or supper meal spread smoked haddock paste on fingers of hot toast and arrange them in a circle around a dish of scrambled eggs. For cocktail parties, use smoked salmon butter, fresh salmon paste, sardine or tunny fish butter, potted cheese, as fillings for the smallest of small sandwiches. Fish, meat and cheese pastes do not combine successfully with vol-au-vent cases, pastry or biscuits, but in sandwiches or spread on fingers of coarse brown bread they will be greeted as a blessed change from sticky canapés and messy dips. Stir a spoonful or two of potted crab or lobster (minus the butter covering) into fresh cream for eggs *en cocotte*, into a béchamel sauce to go over poached eggs or a *gratin* of sole fillets. And as Mrs Johnstone, alias Meg Dods, author of the admirable *Housewife's Manual* of 1826 wrote, 'What is left of the clarified butter (from potted lobster or crab) will be very relishing for sauces' while 'any butter from potted tongue or chicken remaining uneaten will afterwards be useful for frying meat and for pastry for pies'.

CLARIFIED BUTTER

In a large frying or sauté pan put a slab of butter (I use a good quality butter and find that it pays to prepare 2 lb. at a time since it keeps almost indefinitely and is immeasurably superior to fresh butter for frying bread, croquettes, rissoles, fish cakes, veal escalopes, fish *à la meunière* and a score of other tricky cooking jobs). Let the butter melt over very gentle heat. It must not brown, but should be left to bubble for a few seconds before being removed from the heat and left to settle.

Have ready a piece of butter muslin wrung out in warm water, doubled, and laid in a sieve standing over the bowl or deep wide jar in which the butter is to be stored. Filter the butter while it is still warm. For storage keep the jar, covered, in the refrigerator.

The object of clarifying butter is to rid it of water, buttermilk sediment, salt and any foreign matter which (a) for purposes of frying cause the butter to blacken and burn, and (b) render it susceptible to eventual rancidity. The clarification process also expels air and causes the butter to solidify as it cools, making it a highly effective sealing material. In French cookery clarified beef suet, pigs' lard and goose fat are used in precisely the same way to seal pâtés and home-preserved pork and goose. These are the famous *confits* which are the French equivalents of our eighteenth and nineteenth century potted meat, game and poultry. The delicious pork and goose *rillettes* and *rillons* of Western France are also close relations of English potted meats – in other words cooked and shredded or pounded meat packed into pots *after* cooking, as opposed to the pâtés and terrines which are made from raw ingredients cooked directly in the pots or the crust in which they are to be stored and served.

POTTED CHICKEN LIVERS

This is a recipe which produces a rich, smooth and gamey-flavoured mixture, rather like a very expensive French pâté, at a fraction of the price and with very little fuss.

Ingredients are 4 oz. of chicken livers (frozen livers are perfectly adequate); 3 oz. of butter; a tablespoon of brandy; seasonings.

Frozen chicken livers are already cleaned, so if they are being used the only preliminary required is the thawing-out process. If you have bought fresh livers, put them in a bowl of tepid, slightly salted water and leave them for about a couple of hours. Then look at each one very carefully, removing any yellowish pieces, which may give the finished dish a bitter taste.

Heat 1 oz. of butter in a small heavy frying pan. In this cook the livers for about 5 minutes, turning them over constantly. The outsides should be browned but not toughened, the insides should remain pink but not raw. Take them from the pan with a perforated spoon and transfer them to a mortar or the liquidizer goblet.

To the buttery juices in the pan add the brandy and let it sizzle for a few seconds. Pour it over the chicken livers. Add a teaspoon of salt, and a sprinkling of milled pepper. Put in the remaining 2 oz. of butter, softened but not melted. Pound or whizz the whole mixture to a very smooth paste. Taste for seasoning. Press into a little china, glass or glazed earthenware pot or terrine and smooth down the top. Cover, and chill in the refrigerator. Serve with hot crisp dry toast.

If to be made in larger quantities and stored, seal the little pots with a layer of clarified butter, melted and poured over the chilled paste.

Rum (white, for preference) makes a sound alternative to the brandy in this recipe. Surprisingly, perhaps, gin is also very successful.

N.B. Since this dish is a very rich one, I sometimes add to the chicken livers an equal quantity of blanched, poached pickled pork (*not* bacon) or failing pickled pork, a piece of fresh belly of pork, salted overnight, then gently poached for about 30 minutes. Add the cooked pork, cut in small pieces to the chicken livers in the blender.

RILLETTES OR POTTED PORK IN THE FRENCH MANNER

This very famous charcutiers' or pork butchers' speciality is native to Southern Brittany, Anjou and Touraine. It could be described as the French equivalent of our potted meat – although it is very different in texture and taste.

2 lb. of a cheap and fat cut of pork such as neck or belly; 1 lb. of back pork fat; salt; 1 clove of garlic; 2 or 3 sprigs of dried wild thyme on the stalk: a couple of bay leaves; freshly milled black pepper.

Ask your butcher to remove the rind and the bones from the piece of pork meat (the bones can be added to stock and the rind will enrich a beef dish for the next course) and if he will, to cut the back pork fat into cubes.

Rub the meat with salt (about a couple of tablespoons-ful) and let it stand overnight or at least a few hours before cutting it into 1½-inch thick strips – along the grooves left by the bones. Put these strips, and the fat, into an earthenware or other oven dish. In the centre put the crushed clove of garlic, the bay leaf and twig of thyme; mill a little black pepper over the meat and add about half a pint of cold water. Cover the pot. Place it in a very cool oven, gas no. 1, 290°F., and leave for about 4 hours.

Now place a sieve over a big bowl. Turn meat and fat out into the sieve, so that all the liquid drips through. With two forks, pull apart the meat and fat (which should be soft as butter) so that the *rillettes* are shredded rather than in a paste. Pack the *rillettes* lightly into a glazed earthenware or stoneware jar of about ¾ pint capacity (or into two or three smaller jars). Taste for seasoning. Pour over the rillettes (taking care to leave the sediment) enough strained fat to fill the jar. Cool, cover and store in the refrigerator until needed.

Rillettes should be soft enough to spoon out, so remember to remove the jar several hours before dinner. Serve with bread or toast, with or without butter, as you please.

POTTED SALMON

Any woman who has salmon-fishing relations or friends will appreciate the point of this dish. Evolved at a time when salmon was comparatively cheap, and before the days of the tin and the refrigerated larder, potted salmon provided one method (pickling in wine and vinegar, salting, drying, kippering and smoking were others) of preserving surplus fish. Even today there will be readers who will be glad to know of a formula for dealing with a salmon or a piece of one received as a present, too big to be consumed immediately and likely to prove wearisome if eaten cold day after day.

For this recipe, evolved from instructions given in Elizabeth Raffald's *Experienced English Housekeeper* (an admirable book first published in 1769), all you need, apart from fresh salmon, are seasonings of salt, freshly milled white pepper, nutmeg, fresh butter and clarified butter.

Cut the salmon into thinnish steaks, arrange them in one layer in a well-buttered baking dish, sprinkle them with salt and seasonings, add about 1 oz. of fresh butter, cut in pieces, for every pound of salmon, cover the dish with buttered paper and a lid, and put to cook in the centre of a moderately heated oven, gas no. 3, 330°F. In 45 to 50 minutes – a little more or less according to the thickness of the steaks – the salmon will be cooked. Lift the steaks, very carefully, on to a wide sieve, colander, or wire grid placed over a dish so that the cooking butter drains away.

Pack the salmon steaks into a wide dish or pot with the skin side showing. The dish or pot should be filled to capacity without being so crammed that the fish comes higher than the rim of the pot. I make my potted salmon in a shallow round white pot decorated on the outside with coloured fish. It is one of the old dishes especially made for potted char, the freshwater fish once a celebrated delicacy of the Cumberland lake district. Cover with a piece of oiled foil or greaseproof paper and a board, or the base of one of the removable-base tart or cake tins now to be found in many kitchen utensil shops, to fit exactly *inside* the dish. Weight the board. Next day pour in clarified butter to cover the salmon and seal it completely.

Serve potted salmon in its own dish with a cucumber or green salad and perhaps jacket potatoes. A good luncheon or supper dish – and very decorative looking when cut at the table, into the cross-slices of which Elizabeth Raffald notes that 'the skin makes them look ribbed.'

POTTED CRAB

Extract all the meat from a freshly boiled crab weighing about 2 lb. Keep the creamy brown body meat separate from the flaked white claw meat. Season both with salt, freshly milled pepper, mace or nutmeg, cayenne, lemon juice.

Pack claw and body meat in alternate layers in small fire-proof pots. Press down closely. Pour in melted butter just to cover the meat.

Stand the pots in a baking tin of water, cook uncovered on the bottom shelf of a very low oven, gas no. 2, 310°F., for 25 to 30 minutes.

When cold, seal with clarified butter. Serve well chilled.

Potted crab is very rich in flavour as well as in content, and is best appreciated quite on its own, perhaps as a midday dish served only with crisp dry toast, to be followed by a simple lettuce salad or freshly cooked green beans or purple-sprouting broccoli eaten when barely cold, with an oil and lemon dressing.

Those who find crab indigestible may be interested in the advice proffered by Merle's *Domestic Dictionary and Household Manual* of 1842, to the effect that after eating fresh crab it is always advisable to take 'a very small quantity of good French brandy, mixed with its own bulk of water'.

Syllabubs and Fruit Fools

SYLLABUB

It was Herbert Beerbohm Tree's wedding day. His half-brother had been called in to act as best man in place of his real brother who had vanished to Spain. At the celebration breakfast there were syllabubs. Herbert was beguiled by the biblical rhythm of the name. 'And Sillabub, the son of Sillabub reigned in his stead,' he intoned. His stepbrother, half-scandalized and wholly impressed by Herbert's levity, never forgot the episode. He had been ten years old at the time of Herbert's wedding; his name was Max Beerbohm; the story is recounted in Lord David Cecil's *Max, A Biography*;* the date was 1882, and sillabub,† added Max, was then his favourite dish.

Max Beerbohm's generation must have been the last to which the delicious syllabub was a familiar childhood treat. Already for nearly a century the syllabub had been keeping company with the trifle, and in due course the trifle came to reign in the syllabub's stead; and before long the party pudding of the English was not any more the fragile whip of cream contained in a little glass, concealing within its innocent white froth a powerful

---

* Published by Constable, 1964.
† The spelling is Max Beerbohm's.

alcoholic punch, but a built-up confection of sponge fingers and ratafias soaked in wine and brandy, spread with jam, clothed in an egg-and-cream custard, topped with a syllabub and strewn with little coloured comfits. Came 1846, the year that Mr Alfred Bird brought forth custard powder; and Mr Bird's brain-child grew and grew until all the land was covered with custard made with custard powder and the Trifle had become custard's favourite resting-place. The wine and lemon-flavoured cream whip or syllabub which had crowned the Trifle had begun to disappear. Sponge cake left over from millions of nursery teas usurped the place of sponge fingers and the little bitter almond macaroons called ratafias. Kitchen sherry replaced Rhenish and Madeira and Lisbon wines. Brandy was banished. The little coloured comfits – sugar-coated coriander seeds and caraways – bright as tiny tiddly-winks, went into a decline and in their stead reigned candied angelica and nicely varnished glacé cherries.

Now seeking means to combat the Chemicals Age, we look to our forebears for help. We find that the syllabub can replace the synthetic ice cream which replaced the trifle which replaced the syllabub in the first place. The ingredients of a syllabub, we find, are simple and sumptuous. The skill demanded for its confection is minimal, the presentation is basic and elegant. Swiftly, now, before the deep-freezers, the dehydrators and the emulsifiers take the syllabub away from us and return it transformed and forever despoiled, let us discover how it was made in its heyday and what we can do to recapture something of its pristine charm.

In the beginning then, in the seventeenth and eighteenth centuries, there were three kinds of syllabub. There was the syllabub mixed in a punch bowl on a basis of cider or ale and sometimes both, sweetened with sugar and spiced with cinnamon or nutmeg. Into the bowl the milkmaid milked the cow so that the new warm milk fell in a foam and froth on to the cider. The contents of the bowl were left undisturbed for an hour or two, by which time a kind of honeycombed curd had formed on the top, leaving alcoholic whey underneath. Sometimes, on top of the milk curd, a layer of thick fresh cream was poured. This syllabub was more a drink than a whip, a diversion for country parties and rustic festivals.

Co-existing with the syllabub of pastoral England was one made with wine and spirits instead of cider and ale, and with cream instead of milk. This mixture was a more solid one. It was about four-fifths sweetened whipped cream, to be spooned rather than drunk out of the glasses in which it was served, and one-fifth of wine and whey which had separated from the whip, and which you drank when you reached the end of the cream. Then, at some stage, it was discovered that by reducing the proportions of wine and sugar to cream, the whip would remain thick and light without separating. This version was called a solid or everlasting syllabub. One eighteenth-century author, E. Smith, whose *Complete Housewife*, published in 1727, was also the first cookery book to be printed in America, claimed that her Everlasting Syllabubs would remain in perfect condition for nine or ten days, although at their best after three or four.

Not all syllabubs were necessarily made with wine. Sir

Kenelm Digby, whose book of recipes collected from his contemporaries and friends has provided posterity with a graphic record of Stuart cookery, notes that he himself made a fine syllabub with syrup left over from the home-drying of plums; being 'very quick of the fruit and very weak of sugar' this syrup 'makes the Syllabub exceeding well tasted' says Sir Kenelm. He adds that cherry syrup may be used in like manner. In the eighteenth and nine-teenth centuries, syllabubs were sometimes made with the juice of Seville oranges, and in these days we can devise cream and wine or cream and fruit-syrup sylla-bubs to suit ourselves.

My own version of Everlasting Syllabub:

One small glass, or 4 oz, of white wine or sherry, 2 tablespoons of brandy, one lemon, 2 oz. of sugar, ½ pint of double cream, nutmeg.

The day before the syllabub is to be made, put the thinly pared rind of the lemon and the juice in a bowl with the wine and brandy and leave overnight. Next day, strain the wine and lemon mixture into a large and deep bowl. Add the sugar and stir until it has dissolved. Pour in the cream slowly, stirring all the time. Grate in a little nutmeg. Now whisk the mixture until it thickens and will hold a soft peak on the whisk. The process may take 5 minutes, it may take as long as 15. It depends on the cream, the temperature and the method of whisking. Unless dealing with a large quantity of cream, an electric mixer can be perilous. A couple of seconds too long and the cream is a ruined and grainy mass. For a small amount of cream a wire whisk is perfectly satisfactory and just as quick as an electric beater. An old-fashioned wooden chocolate mill or whisk held upright and twirled between the palms of both hands is also a good implement for whisking cream. The important point is to learn to recognize the moment at which the whisking process is complete.

When the cream is ready, spoon it into glasses, which should be of very small capacity (2 to 2½ oz.) but filled to overflowing. Once in the glasses the cream will not spoil nor sink nor separate. As suggested by Sir Kenelm Digby, a tiny sprig of rosemary or a little twist of lemon peel can be stuck into each little filled glass. Keep the syllabubs in a cool place – not in the refrigerator – until you are ready to serve them. They can be made at least two days before they are needed. The quantities given will fill ten small syllabub or custard cups or sherry glasses and will be enough for four to six people. Though circumstances are so changed it is relevant to remember that in their heyday syllabubs were regarded as refreshments to be offered at card parties, ball suppers and at public entertainments, rather than just as a pudding for lunches and dinners, although they did quite often figure as part of the dessert in the days when a choice of sweetmeats, fruits, jellies, confectionery and creams was set out in a formal symmetrical array in the centre of the table. This seems to have been particularly the case in aristocratic Scottish houses in the early decades of the eighteenth century. In *The Household Book of Lady Grisell Baillie 1692 –1733*, edited, with Notes and Introduction, by Robert Scott-Moncrieff, W.S. Edinburgh, 1911, many of the bills of fare for dinners and suppers recorded between 1713 and 1728 featured syllabubs, regardless of the season. On Christmas Day 1715 'w^t 9 of our frinds 14 at table in all' Lady Grisell's dessert consisted of ratafia cream, two dishes of butter and cheese, jacolet [chocolate] walnuts and almonds, apples, stewed pears, chestnuts, 'sillibubs and jellys'. On May 26th 1718 'at Mr Johnstons' the dessert was 'cherries, sillibubs with strawberries, sweet-meats, oranges', and four dishes of milk. The dessert for Lord Anadall's dinner guests on January 29th 1719, '10 at table', was a specially fine affair. The way it was arranged was indicated by Lady Grisell:

Desert

a salver with sweet meats

stewed pears   pistosenuts

butter   cheese

sillibubs and jellies   a lagere salver   sillibubs and jellies

wt sweet meats

cheese   butter

pistache nuts   stweed aples

a salver with sweet meats

At Lord Anadall's supper that night there was lobster and roast lamb (obviously cold), 'a ring w^t wild foull col-lops and pickles etc, brawn, a cold tart, 'two salvers of silibubs and jellies', and two dishes of confections. As always, Lady Grisell's spelling was uniquely her own.

On December 14th 1719 'Super at Mr Cockburn 11 at table 22 persons in al' there were 'eating poset in

cheana [china] high dish at the head of the table, at the
foot a haunch of venison, 'in the midle of the table a
pirimide sillibubs and orang cream in the past, above it
sweet meets dry and wet', on the sides black pudding,
partridge, larks, celery salad 'made and unmade', veal
collops white sauce, '2 boyld pullets w^t persley sauce, in
the midle pickles of other sort than the comon ones.'

It was at about this time that the epergne, a standing
centre-piece with branched supports for the dessert, was
coming into fashion. At the Princess of Wales's at Rich-
mond on July 15th 1720 Lady Grisell noted that the
'Deseart' was 'a big dish in the Midle with connections and
frute only', and on April 12th 1725, at the Duke of Chan-
dos' magnificent house at Canons, near Edgware, with 'A
Duson at Table' there was 'ane Eparn in the Midle'.* Again
in 1727 'We was eight days at Twitenham. We had always
an Eparn in the midle'. It is interesting to note that when
an epergne stood on the table, there were no creams, jellies, or syllabubs in glasses mentioned in the dessert course,
but Lady Grisell herself did not yet possess such an orna-
ment and for her own dinners still served 'sweetmeats and
jelly and sillibubs', curds and cream, pears and apples,
'pistaches and scorcht almonds, Bisket round the milk' in
the old way in separate dishes, in glasses on footed salvers,
and in sweetmeat glasses.†

---

* The editors of the 1971 OED missed Lady Grisell Baillie. Their
earliest mention of an epergne is quoted as 1775.
† For the syllabub, sweetmeat glasses and glass epergnes of the
eighteenth century see Therle Hughes, *Sweetmeat and Jelly Glasses*,
Lutterworth Press, Guildford, 1982.

ENGLISH FRUIT FOOLS

'Our frailties are invincible'. Robert Louis Stevenson

Soft, pale, creamy, untroubled, the English fruit fool is the most frail and insubstantial of English summer dishes. That at any rate is how it should be, and how we like to think it always was. Here the old cookery books interrupt the smooth sequence. The seventeenth- and eighteenth-century writers do describe a number of fruit fools, fools made from gooseberries, raspberries, strawberries, redcurrants, apples, mulberries, apricots, even from fresh figs; but few of these dishes turn out to be the simple cream-enriched purées we know today. Some were made from rather roughly crushed fruit (the French word *foulé*, meaning crushed or pressed must surely have some bearing on the English name), often they were thickened with eggs as well as cream, sometimes they were flavoured with wine and spices, perfumed sugar and lemon peel.

Two hundred years ago it was those recipes listed under the heading of creams which were much more like the fruit fools of today. Evidently, at some stage, it came to be appreciated that the eggs and the extra flavourings were unnecessary, that they even distort the fresh flavour of the fruit. This is especially true of berry fruits and of apricots. Gradually the delicacy now regarded as the traditional English fruit fool came to be accepted as a purée of fruit plus sugar, fresh thick cream, and nothing more.

Like the syllabub, the fruit fool was almost always

114

served in glasses or custard cups, although Susannah MacIver, an Edinburgh cookery teacher and author of an excellent little book called *Cookery and Pastry*, 1774, directs that her gooseberry cream be served on an 'asset', the old Scots word for platter.

From the following few recipes it is easy to see that there was never any *one* method of making English fruit creams and fools, and that over the past three centuries the two have fused. In the process some charming variations have disappeared. Some of these would be worth reviving, for example Robert May's beautiful 'black fruit' mixtures.

In this selection of old and modern recipes I give precedence to those dishes made from the gooseberry, because green gooseberry fool is – to me at any rate – the most delicious as well as the most characteristic of all these simple, almost childlike, English dishes.

GOOSEBERRY FOOL

This is my own method of making gooseberry fool.

2 lb. of green gooseberries; ½ lb. of sugar; a minimum of ½ pint of double cream.

Wash the gooseberries. There is no need to top and tail them. Put them in the top half of a double saucepan with the sugar, and steam them (or if it is easier bake them in a covered jar in a low oven) until they are quite soft. Sieve them through the mouli having first strained off surplus liquid which would make the fool watery. When the purée is quite cold add the cream. More sugar may be necessary.

Later in the season when gooseberries are over, delicious fools can be made with uncooked strawberries; a mixture of raspberries and redcurrants, also uncooked; and blackberries, cooked as for gooseberries; but in this case I think that cream spoils the rich colour of the fruit and should be offered separately.

To me it is essential to serve fruit fools in glasses or in simple white cups, and with shortbread or other such biscuits to go with them.

BLACK FRUIT FOOL OR BLACK TART STUFF

This is a recipe adapted from a dish evidently popular three hundred years ago in the days of the Stuarts, when a purée of dried prunes, raisins and currants cooked in wine was used as a filling for tarts and pies. Recipes for this 'black tart stuff' as it was called appear in at least two cookery books of the second half of the seventeenth century. One of these books, *The Accomplisht Cook* of 1660 is a most beautiful piece of cookery literature. The author, Robert May, worked in a number of grand and noble households, including that of the Countess of Kent, whose book of medical receipts appeared posthumously in 1653 under the title *A Choice Manual, Or Rare Secrets in Physick and Chirurgery*. Published together with *A Choice Manual* was a little book of cookery receipts entitled *A True Gentlewoman's Delight*, often also attributed, although probably wrongly, to the Countess of Kent.

Robert May gives several different variations on his 'black tart stuff' recipe, one of which includes damsons.

A True Gentlewoman's Delight also gives a formula for black tart stuff. My own version is the result of experiments with these different recipes. I find it a delicious and refreshing cold fruit purée. As a pie filling it is rich and dark without the cloying and heavy qualities of mincemeat. It has also a certain originality which provides a small surprise at the end of the meal.

Exact proportions of the different dried fruits are not important, but as a rough guide, use ½ lb. of good large prunes, ¼ lb. of raisins (Spanish muscatels are the best for flavour and colour, stoneless Australian or South African raisins are cheaper) and 2 oz. of currants, plus ¼ pint of red table wine or ⅛ pint of port.

Put the prunes in an earthenware oven dish, with the wine and enough water to cover them. Leave them, in the covered pot, in a very slow oven, anything from gas no. ½ to 1 or 290°F., to gas no. 3 or 330°F., for 2 to 3 hours or longer, until they are very swollen and completely soft and have absorbed most of the liquid. During the final hour or so of cooking put the raisins and currants previously well washed, in a separate oven pot, and with water to cover them, to bake.

Stone the prunes, sieve them, with any remaining juice. Strain and discard the water from the raisins and currants. Sieve them. Mix the two purées together.

Serve well chilled in glasses, or in one large bowl, with a layer of thin pouring cream floated on the top, and with sponge or shortbread fingers.

When the purée is made a little extra port can be added by those who like a stronger flavour of wine.

These quantities fill six glasses of about 3-oz. capacity.

The purée keeps well in the refrigerator, so it is economical to make a batch and store it.

A note for teetotallers: I have several times eaten another modern version of this dish in which black coffee rather than wine is used for flavouring the dried fruit.

······· GREAT 🐧 FOOD ·······

LOVE IN A DISH
& OTHER PIECES
M. F. K. Fisher

M. F. K. FISHER'S PERSONAL, intimate culinary
essays are well-loved American classics, combining
recipes with her anecdotes, reminiscences, cultural
observations and passionate storytelling.

Hailed as 'poet of the appetites' by John Updike
and considered the greatest American prose writer by
W. H. Auden, Fisher saw eating as inextricably bound
up with living well. Whether reflecting on an epic lunch
served by a fanatical waitress, the life-giving properties
of wine, quails whose glorious smell 'would rouse Lazarus'
or how the love of food can save a marriage, each
piece is a perfectly crafted work of art.

'Poet of the appetites'
JOHN UPDIKE

GREAT FOOD

RECIPES AND LESSONS FROM A DELICIOUS COOKING REVOLUTION
Alice Waters

A CHAMPION OF ORGANIC, locally produced and seasonal food and founder of acclaimed Californian restaurant Chez Panisse, Alice Waters has recently been awarded the *Légion d'honneur* in France for her contributions to food culture. In this book, she explores the simplest of dishes in the most delicious of ways, with fresh, sustainable ingredients a must, even encouraging cooks to plant their own garden.

From orange and olive salad to lemon curd and ginger snaps, Waters constantly emphasizes the joys and ease of cooking with local, fresh food, whether in soups, salads or sensual, classic desserts.

'Waters is a legend'
JAY RAYNER

GREAT FOOD

THROUGHOUT the history of civilization, food has been livelihood, status symbol, entertainment – and passion. The twenty fine food writers here, reflecting on different cuisines from across the centuries and around the globe, have influenced each other and continue to influence us today, opening the door to the wonders of every kitchen.